# Fall of the House of Dad

# *Fall of the House of Dad*

## MY DIVORCE JOURNEY FROM LOSS TO JOY

JOHN OAKLEY MCELHENNEY

press of light and space

Austin, Texas

# Contents

**WE CARRY ON. WE DO BETTER. WE KEEP GOING.**

# Introduction – Why Tell This Story?

In divorce, the man often is the parent asked to leave the house and leave the rest of the family as undisturbed as possible. I get it. We are trying to lessen the impact of the divorce on the kids. But…what about the dad? As they continued on in some sort of "Daddy's on a business trip" mode, I was immediately homeless and alone. It is quite different for us dads. This is a fragment of my journey, offered as an honest reflection of my loss and eventual return to hopeful and happy.

I have written about my divorce since the beginning of the experience, even before I was actually out of the house or divorced. But the process begins the minute you realize your partner is no longer in it with you. For any number of reasons, they have moved on, and from the moment you are told about the new horizon, a future without you, you begin your journey.

Mine was a journey of loss, depression, recovery, self-discovery, and a renewed commitment to becoming an even better parent than I had been. My kids needed me more now, even as I was less available to them. And it was my responsibility to keep the sadness and anger as part of my experience and not theirs. In this way I started The Off Parent as an anonymous blog in the fall of 2010, after my divorce became final in August.

Nine years later, my resilience and confidence are high. I am not sad about what has passed. I am grateful that I have been able to feel and grow through the devastating experience of becoming a divorced dad. My joy and positive approach may not be directly captured in these pages, though I will close with a taste of where I am now.

This is my divorce song. I am singing for survival and hope. I have passed through the gates of hell and lived to sing about it. If you are going through a divorce at this moment, I am sorry. I hope that my experience gives you some comfort and hope. I pray that you suffer less and yet experience everything you need to allow your life to be transformed. Divorce is the worst thing that ever happened in my life. But now, as I am somewhat resurrected, I know the loss burned away everything that was unnecessary. I am lean, mean, and happier than I have ever been. I am alone, sure, but I have my focus where it belongs, on my kids and their lives, their welfare. And in a physical way, I am still connected to my ex-wife. I wish her only happiness. I realize this book has the potential to be hurtful. I decided the release and potential for healing from revealing this story for others to learn from outweighed the risk.

To my ex-wife: May you find happiness.

To my kids: When you are old enough to uncover this book, may you understand yourselves a bit more by hearing the story I could never tell you.

# ENDINGS ARE ALSO BEGINNINGS

I am attempting to bring some structure and organization to the story of my house struggles and depression that were whipped back into full gear as I experienced the crushing effects of divorce on my personal and financial stability. It began the moment she said she was done.

# A Once and Future King

The loss of my kingdom. I don't think it's a particularly male thing, imagining your house and neighborhood as a kingdom. I think we all feel a sense of protection and pride around our homesteads. We invest a lot of time and energy in providing a comfortable existence for ourselves and our families.

It is not a happy thing to be exiled from your kingdom. Everything that goes with it. Kids, pets, comfortable bed, study areas, entertainment, warmth, yards, play. Everything comes to an end.

What once was a WE provide is now an I provide. And I have not been so lucky in terms of the next chapter in my working life. I've made money. I've worked. But I am essentially homeless at the moment. Being shut out of my house meant that I could either buy a completely new residence in our neighborhood or...leave.

The blessing is that I have a sister in the city who had a mother-in-law plan available. And it came with built-in kids, her 12-year-old twins, a boy and a girl. And for that I am glad.

But I have no privacy. The TV is a constant irritation, as the largest one sits directly on the other side of my bedroom door. And of course, 90% of my stuff is still in my ex-wife's house. I don't have a place to put it. And I get to be thankful that she's not insisting that I get a storage unit.

I know that I will return to a kingdom of my own. And I will make a way again in the world of empowered work, but for now it is difficult. As fall is now moving in and the weather is changing, I long for a

place to relax and be alone. And an opportunity to begin the rebuilding process.

# She Would've Liked Me to Just Leave the House

When the proverbial shit hit the fan, and she had fully articulated that she wanted a divorce, that she had gone to see an attorney to understand her "options," that even our therapist had shown his doubts about our survivability, she wanted me to leave. She was incensed that I simply would not LEAVE THE HOUSE.

I made a declaration over and over as she kept raising the subject. "I will not bring this divorce full-force into this house until our kids have finished this year in school." She was not happy. She used ideas like "trial separation" as enticements. No way.

I was the survivor of a horrible divorce, when my parents started the kid wars that became my life. When I grieved my divorce, as it had been spelled out for me by my sessions with the ex, I was crying for my kids, not for me. Of course, I'm aware enough to know that my tears were really tears AS A SON for another son who was losing his dad. I lost my dad, big time. When he walked out that door, the second time, he never came back. And our lives quickly descended into a living hell for years. My dad is not me. My son is not having that experience. Not by a long shot.

But I was not willing to uproot the entire family simply because the ex had come to a decision, had weighed her options, and had seen an opening and a greener pasture outside my arms. Our kids were in second and fourth grades. It still makes me angry to think she was so oblivious to their needs and only focused on HER needs.

Her needs for immediate separation and space. To get HER house. I guess...

I did not move out until the kids were done with the school year. It was two of the hardest months of my life, knowing I was toast, that my wife was unreachable, and that I was more of a ghost dad than a dad. But I stood my ground. Fuck her and her separation and space. And fuck if I was going to give her the house, just like that.

In the end, that's what happened, she got the house, as my real estate friend who was experienced in several divorces said she would. "She's gonna get the house, and you're still going to be paying for it," he said. While part of that does not seem fair, it's the way it is. Any whining about it is whining. Let's move on.

I did not walk out the door that March. But in many ways, as June arrived and the kids completed their semester in elementary school, I suffered mightily for my decision. I think it was the right decision. As I said to the ex, it's a business. We can't just divorce overnight. There are a lot of details to work out. So what's the hurry? Other than the fact that you want me out, you want to start whatever is next. (And boy didn't she. She was sexing it up within weeks of the divorce papers being filed. SHE WAS THE STARVED PARTY? What? That's kinda funny.)

Okay, so I stayed and now I have my badge of honor and my heart-on-sleeve righteousness. But it was a hard two months as we navigated sleeping in separate rooms, getting the kids ready for school, and coordinating the details of running a family. By June I was a basket case. I was depressed beyond belief, I was hardly functional, but hey, we'd done it. The kids got to finish second and fourth grade without the stigma or trauma of their familial collapse.

I'm trying to take precautionary action this year, before June arrives with its regret and memories. The long summer. The death of my marriage. The real separation of my kids from me. And the last three summers have been very hard. I can plan, strategize, and keep meeting with my talky doctor, but to say I'm bulletproof heading towards summer would be a fool's dream.

I am leery of summer now. I am a bit sad just now, thinking about how hard the past three summers have been.

I am also strong, rebuilt, and reoriented towards health, fitness, and being a great parent. And part of that includes looking after the best interests of our kids, even when it goes against what we want or think we need.

# FIRST CHALLENGES: MONEY & DEPRESSION

One of the first challenges, if money is an issue, is establishing a new home, a place where you can begin being a dad again. How long it takes to reestablish this residence depends a lot on your mental state of mind and your employment situation. In my case both were significantly damaged. I moved into my sister's spare bedroom. This might have been a saving grace, as I was not ready to be fully alone. When I was "off," I had my sister and her two kids to keep me company. My story became, "And I didn't need to be alone. I was so lucky."

# Followed by the Black Dog (of Depression)

He came out of nowhere with a grin and a wild look in his brown eyes. The black dog began following me this morning on my walk. He seemed lonely for someone to cruise around with, and he took my singing with the iPod as encouragement. And he was like a shadow.

So much of the time recovering from divorce is about recovering from depression. "Clinical" or "temporary" depression is a bitch. It keeps you in bed when you should go to work. It makes you eat crap when you should really start watching what you eat even more carefully. And for me, the worst part, is it makes me isolate like a motherfucker. That's the killer for me.

I'm not depressed at the moment. So I am able to see and respond to the black dog [sadness] with an open hand. My energy level is high, I'm walking, so that's good, and the music is weaving its tentacles in my brain, and I'm feeling quite buoyant at the moment. So where did the black dog come from?

One of the most pivotal moments in recovery is admitting to yourself that depression is a problem. For me, isolation is pretty deep on the list of symptoms. By the time I'm isolating and fucking up at work, the other mechanics of depression are in full bloom.

**My positive check-ins** look kind of like this:

- eating

- sleeping
- sexual desire (even masturbation can be a positive sign)
- laughing or playing
- calling people back
- spending time with friends

When any of these balance points gets way out of whack, I'm heading towards a wrestling match with the black dog. The last real battle lasted four to five months and easily could've killed me.

So when the black dog of depression shows up, I try to take evasive action as soon as I can.

**Evasive actions**:

- go for a walk
- play a game (online with others if I can't be with real people)
- clean up my diet (it's amazing what junk food and sugar highs can do to your overall life performance)
- see if there's anything pornographic that interests me (if I can get an erection, at least I know I'm alive, I have a desire)
- call one of my divorce-buddies ("Um, I'm just calling because I don't want to call, and I don't want to get together for lunch or anything.")
- meet with my counselor or doctor (talky therapists are critical, and meds doctors are too, if you've ever had deep bouts of depression)

The most important thing for me is to stay out of the isolation chamber. That is where I slowly, patiently kill myself.

So this morning, I'm not feeling much charge from the depressive side of my life at the moment, and the black dog is more of a friend and companion. He won't come close enough for me to pet him, but he smiles at me just the same. He keeps his distance, I keep singing along to the music on my iPod, and we mosey on down the road together.

And then out of nowhere appears another set of black dogs. The twins from down the street. These guys I know.

For a minute I'm not sure if the black dog is going to gel or fight, but I keep walking, imagining they're going to work it out between themselves.

I look back about five minutes later to see if the black dog is still with me. The three dogs are doing some sort of ecstasy-daisy-chain-circle-dance. They are lost in their dog-ness.

I am happy the black dog has found better companions. I'm not afraid to befriend him. The converse is true. Depression is part of loss. And if you are FEELING the divorce, you probably will feel depressed.

For me, my blog became one of my re-stabilizing forces. I write to process. I write to learn and make sense of what is happening. The first time, when my ex asked me to take the blog down, I was depressed. What I realized only later was that I was in the early stages of depression. By shutting down the expression of my anger, sadness, and loss, by killing the blog the first time, I actually hastened my own slip further into darkness.

Today the black dog (of depression) is my friend. I will see him again from time to time. He will travel with me for a bit. And we will part ways when one of us has a more interesting opportunity.

# How Much Longer Until I Feel Better? (Post-Divorce Depression)

One a day, or one day at a time, is the only way to think about recovery from divorce. Recently a trusted friend said that we DO need to take vitamins, that there are some key elements (in the general population's diet) we just don't get from our diet any more. And while I'm certain she was thinking of something more holistic than one-a-days, the price and convenience were right.

Each day, I dutifully swallow these little green happy pills. And I can't help but wonder, "When are these new minerals and vitamins going to kick in? When will I feel better?" (Of course, if you need real happy pills, be sure and talk to your doctor.)

There is no map out of this land of confusion. You press on, day after day, because you must, because there are people (kids in my case) counting on you.

There are going to be good days and bad days. And even when you feel completely free of the influence of your exy, something will happen, a trigger, a song, a restaurant, a movie, that will trigger you feelings of longing and loss again. It's okay, it's good to embrace those deep feelings in the moment and then move on past them.

For me, the routine is the thing. I'm usually up by 6:00 a.m. when I do my creative writing. I developed this habit when I needed time to write; I would wake up before the entire house to get an hour in before I needed to wake up everyone else. It was always a little like being Santa Claus. Everyone was soundly dreaming away and I was up making coffee and lunches and sitting in my comfy chair and writing. It was a golden moment.

I enjoyed the routine of getting the kids out the door every day for school. I was the Breakfast Dad. And I'm sure, from what my kids tell me, things are a bit different at the old house now. My son told me he shared with my ex about how I get them up in plenty of time to listen to some music and roll around in bed before having to get dressed. There's always music in my house.

So now there are four or five days in a row when I don't have them to wake up, when they are with their mom. I still get up at 6:00 a.m. and write. And even by myself, even on weekends, I love this time alone. I think this blog, this writing about it, has brought me up and out of any lingering sadness completely. Not so sure about the One-a-Day vitamins. I think my friend was imagining a more holistic vitamin. (grin)

So I'm up and at it early every day. Now that it's getting really damn hot during the day, I try and get my walk in before 10:00 a.m. as well. There is no question that the walking has helped a lot. Not with my Buddha belly (yet) but certainly with the energy and confidence that comes from "doing what's good for you."

And today, just for a moment, speaking to my son on the phone, I wanted to be with him rather than where I was. I could've changed my day and done something else with him, but instead I stuck with the plan. I do have to get the work done so I can keep the house, and keep making child support payments, and eventually catch up on my taxes and credit cards. Onward we go.

And walking down the road or trail with my iPod blasting, I can imagine that I will come through all of this in a better place. (Hey, maybe that One-a-Day is working.)

# Depression Is No Joke: Suicide Is Not the Answer to any Question or Problem

As I'm thinking about some of the darkest times in my life, the fall from having it all to having nothing was the harshest thing I could imagine. There were moments...

(**Disclaimer:** I am not a counselor or mental health professional. I am not offering advice on how to treat your depression or suicidal thoughts. I am saying GET HELP and GET IT NOW.)

For now, here are a few things I learned about depression.

Your brain is fooling you. You can no longer trust your own thoughts. Even the negative thoughts are not accurate. What was critically important for me was to realize when I was getting depressed and go into humorous observation mode. "Wow, my thinking is really fucked up." There's nothing funny about depression, but sometimes if I could amplify my dark clouds to the ultimate extreme I could remind myself how silly my thinking could get. I mean, I was probably not responsible for nuclear war. But that's how it felt sometimes.

Soft thoughts about suicide are actually suicidal thoughts. Harder to admit the word "suicide" into my vocabulary. But I had vague ideas about jumping from a bridge or crashing my car at high speed. Those are called "ideation" but ARE actually suicidal thoughts. Take them seriously. Again, remember, your brain is crazy at this point. Even odd thoughts about how you "might" kill yourself are actually thoughts about killing yourself. I know that sounds kind of circular, but it's easy to discount the "concept" rather than the "plan" of killing yourself.

Tell your care team about your "ideation." Even the littlest thing can be a clue into what's going on in your brain. And once you get over the hurdle of talking about it, you can begin to disassemble the issues and problems that are making you consider that ending your life might be a solution to ANYTHING. It's not a solution!

If you ever find yourself with a suicidal plan, call 911. Do whatever it takes to get yourself to share your planning with someone else. This is serious. If you have a plan, call your healthcare provider now. If your plan is in motion, call 911. Only you can take the action to prevent this.

Everything else can wait. Everything else, every problem, every situation can wait for you to clear your depressive thoughts. You can do a lot of helpful things to move forward and out of depression. I have some powerful references in the library. But for now, just know that ANYTHING you do to stop your depressive acting out is worth it. Ice cream, funny movies, computer games, whatever it takes to break the spiral of dark thoughts.

Isolation is your enemy. Those dark thoughts can seethe and spin unchecked when you are staying in bed or blocking and not returning phone calls. What you need, but can't seem to ask for, is companionship. Just another soul to be with, to check in, to ask, "What are you doing tomorrow?" Do what you can to find that one person who understands. And then thank them for providing you with a check-in. That's all you need at first, a check-in. Someone who is going to call and whom you cannot block. It sucks, but the longer you dig into the darkness, the harder it is to pull out.

In my case I used some of the 12-Step literature to help bootstrap myself back out of my dark cave and into recovery. The concept of MASSIVE ACTION really spoke to me. The idea was that little incremental steps were not going to be enough to pull me up out of depression. So I signed up for a divorce recovery class (10-week counselor-led group) and joined an Aikido class. And every day, I made a plan to get out of bed and out in the world for a healthy lunch.

Just beginning these commitments toward health signaled to my depression that I was not going to take it lying down any more.

Some people have the idea that depression is a weakness. That everybody should be able to pull themselves up if they wanted to. Fuck that. Depression is a real beast. If you've never felt the weight of the black beast on you, you are lucky. But if you have dealt with, or think you may be dealing with depression, GET HELP.

You don't have to do it alone. And trying to do it ALONE might make things even worse. The shame of depression is still real. But you cannot let it prevent you from getting the help you need.

# Loneliness. Fessing Up When Things Hurt for No Apparent Reason

Today was one of those days. Nothing really happened to make me sad, but dropping the happy bubbling kids off at the ex-wife's house today, I felt the depth of pain again. Maybe I have to come clean, maybe I need to look at my loneliness for a minute rather than skate over it in the name of exhaustion, too much work, apathy, and entertainment.

I don't want to write about missing my kids. I want to go off and queue up a Game of Thrones episode and relax and forget about it.

I felt the pang of anxiety for the first time in months last week. I was dialing in some financial details and realized the bulk of the work that was materializing two months ago had still failed to produce the steady income I needed. So I'm back against the wall, it's the new month, and I still owe half of last month's child support payment.

It is hard to share that. I'd rather curl up and be depressed. Maybe this is too raw, unedited... I can feel the emptiness and hopelessness that comes as part of this new planet I have landed upon. Perhaps the voice can come through and punch me back into gear.

Over the last two weeks, the anger, vibrancy, and passion have veered off course into self-doubt and sadness.

Checklist:

1. Exercise. YES
2. Eating well. MARGINAL
3. Sleeping well. YES
4. Keeping up with work. MARGINAL
5. Loneliness quotient: VERY HIGH

Dammit. I do not want to be here. I've called my support team. I am looking at what is going on with attention to ACTION rather than RUMINATION. And now as the sun is going down, I'm gonna have the second walk of the day. A short one, an appreciation.

I've fallen down, but I am also in the process of getting up. Again. We get up again.

# Feeling Again or Not Feeling Again

See if you can feel the irony of this. I am picking up my kids after school at my former house. And the dogs have gotten into the trash in the kitchen. So what do I do, clean it up? Make it a little more messy? Ignore it, not my problem?

Well, she is nice enough to let me use the house as a pick-up zone. It's good for the kids. So I do a partial pick up of coffee grounds and trash off the kitchen floor. Sweep but not mop.

So we're waiting 20 minutes for me to take my daughter to Brownies. My ex had a business trip and it IS my day. We hustle up to the playground, and no one is in sight. We drive over to the park, and it is completely empty. Turns out they are at the playground but inside the neighborhood association building. We figure this out about 20 minutes into the meeting.

The plan was for my son and I to do a quick grocery run while my daughter was doing Brownie scouts. Problem was, by the time we got her to the right room, only 30 minutes remained in the meeting. We couldn't get to the store and back in 30 minutes. So my son and I were left to our own devices. He drew and I fuddled with my Blackberry and wished it had a real browser. I tuned into all the beautiful women coming to the playground with new offspring. Oh yeah.

So at the same park where I was a den leader with my son in Cub Scouts, I was now simply waiting in the park on a beautiful day, looking at beautiful women, and grooving on the pictures my son was drawing.

I guess we could have gone back to the house. It's HER house now, but it will always be "the" house. Much of me is still inside.

And I give thanks that my ex is not bitter and angry or she'd have my shit in a storage unit. As it is, I am still looking for a place to live, and all of my furniture and most of my clothes still in her house. She's been boxing and moving some stuff. But lots of me still remains, almost trapped, until I can find my own house.

# Since My Last Confession

It's been awhile. Um, and I'd like to tell you it's been pleasant or productive. It has had moments, but mostly I fell off a cliff.

Overwhelmed with sadness and longing after divorce.

I'm not sure exactly what kicked in to release the flood of...Depression, Fear, Lonliness... I put them all with capital letters, because it has been a bear crawling back out of the abyss. I fully expected, as I closed my last post, to pick things up and stick with the honest revelations. And... NOT. My creative flow doesn't work that way. And I simply shut it all down.

In some ways I was crashing back into my divorce again. The rage that I expressed on my blog (and now in these pages) turned into feelings of shame and regret. Why would I vent so furiously? I must've been nuts putting this much emotion and pain out there. How embarrassing.

What now has changed my mind? What elements of life have brought me back to life? There is so much to tell.

Let's start about the time the wheels fell off. I was struggling to finish my last blog post ("Loneliness. Fessing Up When Things Hurt for No Apparent Reason"), was fairly self-aware of what was happening, and still was unable to avert the plummet. It wasn't one thing that was freaking me out, it was several.

The biggest fear factor for me was money. What I thought I had a month before had failed to materialize. And I went from self-confident (and perhaps arrogant) to despondent and lost. When the ability to pay your credit cards begins to fall off the map, things get a bit stressful. And they had been falling off for months. The prospect of work was keeping me afloat. And as the client continued to stall, my grip on the positive side of EVERYTHING began to loosen.

It wasn't a dramatic pop, more of a sigh, as I let go of the cliff of Maslow's hierarchy and slipped back into the base plan of survival. Trips to pick up the kids at my former house became harder. My longing for a woman who did not love me back continued to fester, even in the contradiction of my own awareness and good counseling. And my desperation about my own situation, probably emotional more than financial, began to turn bleak indeed.

I laughed at my irrational mind as I walked through our upscale grocery store. On one side of the unattainable relationship model was the yoga-fresh women in their mid-morning workout stride, flashing teeth, thin and evolved athletic legs, and Lulu Lemon outfits that cost more than my car payment. And on the other side was the obese cleaning lady standing in the customer service line. Neither extreme seemed attainable. And thus I felt hopeless in my contemplations of how I would EVER find a woman, another woman, to be with. I wanted to crawl back into what I knew before. To collapse in the sturdiness of my ex-wife, regardless of the cost.

So I was out of my mind.

And I could not seem to put any of the puzzle pieces of my life back together again. So I did what I do. I isolated. I shut down. I became very quiet. But I was hoping to be found and rescued. I knew that. I was nose diving into "fuck you" while hoping for a hand to reach out and scoop me up. I was emotionally about five years old.

# What I Wanted – "Responsible Separation"

"What can we do to give you the distance you need, without hurting the family?"

He kept saying, "I don't love you anymore." And "I don't like what you've become."

She kept saying, "I don't buy it."

The gender roles are reversed for me in this situation, but these words were those of Laura A. Munson writing in the *New York Times* about her husband's request for a divorce.

WOW.

So she committed to her happiness, regardless of what external circumstances brought her, and said "No" to her husband's request. And she offers some interesting wisdom that I know I need to grok more fully.

I had become the keystone in my ex's anger. And my questions regarding her rage, and did she think she was going to turn into a happy person, simply by me walking out the door? I don't think she really ever responded to my question. But perhaps I wasn't asking. I was telling. And I was NOT agreeing to walk out the door.

That's what I was striving for, but perhaps I turned it into a marital fight without meaning to. Yes I pressed, but I was exhausted about being held at arm's length from the love of my life and trapped in the box of indecision. It wasn't the sex, it was the simple expressions of caring that were difficult for her. A warmth that I had come to crave was being withheld.

# Flat-Out Broke: Money Survival Basics After Divorce

How is it possible? I'm a successful professional in my 49th year of life and I have a negative balance in my checking account and $14 in my retirement account? And even more amazing, how is it that I am not freaking out?

Since the full child support payments kicked in, I have been scrambling not to bounce checks. I'm astounded by the amount of money I am now paying to my ex-wife. I know it's "for the kids" and all, but I am barely keeping gas in my car and food in my belly at this moment. Much less food in my kids' bellies and the occasional splurge, eating out or going out to see a movie.

I am lucky, too, as I have a high earning potential, and even in this dropped economy I've made a reasonable, though severely reduced, income. And my ex has remained fully employed since about three months before the divorce was final. (Go figure that?)

I've got some new clients and good financial forecasts for next month. But it always takes a while for new business to ramp up to full hours. I'm close, and I have invoices out to be paid, but at the moment I can't buy a Starbucks coffee. Oh, and I forgot to mention my three credit cards, useless burdens at this point. Another source of frustration. But I'll get to them as well.

Of course, the kids come first. Of course they do. And I will say it to myself again and again, "I want my kids to have a healthy life." And

I have to believe I will rise above the cash drain with a significant uptick in my income. That's about all I have, the faith that I will dig out from under this.

Once I got over the shock of not being able to pay all of my bills, I started researching strategies to survive. Here's what I learned.

The bankruptcy/debt counselors really only have one solution: consolidate your debt and agree to a payment plan. Um, this does not work when your income is ZERO.

The counselor did say one very valuable thing. "At some point you will run out of things to sell off, and you will have to make a decision about what bills to pay."

My decisions revolved around a few things:

- I wanted to keep my house. (Mortgage payments were a critical path.)

- I had to eat and drive to work. (Groceries and gas were non-negotiables.)

- I needed electricity, water, and high-speed internet access to do my work and live comfortably.

- I committed to the child support payments, and I was going to pay them. (I did negotiate a deferral on also paying the kid's health insurance until my work re-stabilized.)

Other than that, every other expense, bill, financial obligation was on hold. Paused. Put in a file and forgotten about. I could not pay my credit cards for the first time in my life. Okay, I'm over it. Ignore the calls. I had to tell my ex that I could not pay the health care but that I would make good on the debt as soon as I had positive cash flow. I had to negotiate the timing on my payments to my ex so I could make two payments during the month.

And then I have continued to work like hell to get my work situation back to full productivity. Yes, the economy is hard. I've had a lot of interviews but no offers. And my consulting business has kept me alive for almost a year since my last full-time job.

But the bottom line is, I'm surviving. I've cut back to the bare basics. And today I've still got nothing. I can't take my kids to the movies tonight. And the groceries in the fridge are what we've got until they go back to their mom's on Monday.  And IT IS OKAY. It's not fun, but it's workable. The clients will pay, the credit cards will eventually get back on a payment plan, and the ex will get her full legally awarded child support.

In the meantime, my job is not to thrash, not to share the stress of this trying moment with my kids, and to carry on. It sucks some-times. And I'm not 100% sure being the non-custodial parent was a good move for me financially. BUT, today it's what I've got.

Hi Ho, Hi Ho!

**Update:** A new reader tweeted at me today about this post. It made her hot under the collar. "Paying child support is not heroic," she said. She missed the gist of this post. Yes, we are both struggling with money issues. But I was at ZERO. Not by some bad behavior or fatal flaw. Not because I was not looking for work.

# Love and War; It's all Here – Seeking Love and Peace

A contrast and comparison of the two most powerful letters I've written this year.

1. Love letter to the silent "woman with potential" (partial). Responding to an email she sent me about why she hasn't been able to see me over the last two weeks.

+++
*Sweet* [woman's name], *(i like the sound of that)*
*I completely understand.*
*If the moment is casual and easy and without expectations, maybe it would be easier to just include me in an activity you're already going to do. No prep or primp, just, "Hey, I'm going for a walk at 2:00, wanna go?" Imagining some of the resistance is merely the additional effort required to include someone else, someone who's "checkin you out."*
*But that's an easy one to interrupt, right? Just time together, that's my goal. Intentionality is useful in many situations, but here, I'm easy and free of expectations.*
*And me:*
*1. I can be more invitive (invite-y), but I feel this adds pressure rather than enticement. And thus patience and peace of mind is my repose.*
*2. Thrilled with the idea of* [woman's name].
*3. Happy.*
*4. Intentional when it makes sense.*
*At the moment it appears it doesn't fit. That's okay. I can imagine you are frazzled and adding ONE MORE FKIN THING, even if that thing is*

*magically delicious, is too much.*
*Here I AM. As long as it's okay for me to ping you every now and then to check-in, I can mind my own mind. And when there is an opening on your end for more... Well...*
*Final thought: I loved, love, will love getting your messages in the future, and I will respond in kind.*
+++




2. Declaration of Independence from the ex-wife's continuing drama about money.

+++

*Money.*
*What I can tell you.*

1. *You are going to get every penny you are owed. Any language from you about "collecting" or "enforcement" now makes me laugh rather than get mad. It's absurd. Maybe it's your dad speaking, but there is no DEFAULT on my child support.*

2. *If there is a perception from the kids that money is flowing, it's a misperception, maybe due to my joy in life at the moment.*

3. *After my mortgage and base necessities, **you and the kids are my first priority**.*

4. *Work is good. And it does look like I will get several new pieces of business that should speed up my catch-up.*

5. *A month that I am able to afford a housekeeper is a good month. But that $100 has no bearing on your payments.*

6. *I am not spending ANY money on myself, after food, shelter and internet.*

*What I cannot tell you.*

1. *Timing or schedule of my payments through the summer. I simply don't have the information myself.*

2. *Exact amounts you can expect through the summer.*

*If you have doubts about me ever getting caught up, those are based on fear and not reality. I will do my best to inform you of when money is coming in and what portion of every income event you can count on. But until the check is in my hand from my other clients, I will not guess at dates and schedules.*
*There will come a day when the money and schedule are easy and predictable. I am working towards that with 100% of my efforts.*
*That's the best I can do.*
+++

Maybe I could do more, better, try harder, but I don't think so.

The real story is that my life is good. In spite of being in arrears with Wells Fargo and the ex. I am working plenty. I am landing new business. I am keeping my head out of the gutter of depression around the pressure of money and lack of money.

Here's the rub.

When we were married, I worked as a freelance consultant for years. I was successful, and then 9-11 took the prosperity right out of my self-employment. What ultimately forced me to seek FTE (full-time employee) status was (1) the need for my family to have robust healthcare coverage, and (2) the ex's unwillingness to get a full-time full-pay job herself. Of course in the early part of our kids' lives, that was by design, but towards the end of our marriage, her unwillingness almost felt like defiance. Case in point, the last full year of our marriage she actually had a negative income after taxes and expenses were taken out. How's that for escalating the stress levels. Of course, the party line was I was the one with the "employment" problem.

Now, however, in divorce, the ex must have full-time employment. And with that comes the opportunity to put the kid's healthcare on her policy. Still bill it to me, but give them the access to healthcare, which these days still requires a FTE status to acquire. As a result, the opportunity to become a self-employed consultant is possible for me again. She really doesn't have any say about that.

I would've liked to have provided enough financially for her not to work at all while the kids were in elementary school. We did the best we could, and she averaged 15–30 hours a week for a good portion of that time. But as the kids got older, the expectation was that she would start contributing to the overall household growth again.

And the most amazing thing. When she decided she wanted to divorce me, she created a job with a firm owned by some personal friends. When she was required to work, she was very good at it. And when she desired to go to FTE status, it was a quick and decisive event.

Today, when I'm working my flexible schedule, I wonder how easier it would be if we (my child support) were not paying on two houses. How we both might have enjoyed a more flexible lifestyle had we stayed together.

That was not the choice we made. Today she is the FTE. And while I am paying the healthcare costs, and the equivalent of two mortgages (and I will get caught up), she is still in some sort of crisis about money. Seems like this was a pattern in our marriage, too. She was in crisis about something most of the time.

I am not.

And yet the contrast could not be more obvious.

She: has $30K or more in her retirement accounts, little or no credit card debt, and equity in the marital home in the neighborhood of $50k–70k.

Me: spent all of my retirement savings to live and gain access to home ownership again, have no credit cards and bad credit, am behind on my mortgage.

Yet still. I am very happy and optimistic that I am pulling out of this. And I am trying to reassure her, just as I did when we were married, that there will be enough. "We're gonna be fine."

She is stressed to the max, thrashing against me for money and convinced I am the answer and cause of her distress.

I can maintain my neutrality. I can try and respond with kindness rather than anger. I will continue to focus on the happiness and well-being of my kids. The happiness and well-being of my ex were not things I could manage then, and I certainly cannot manage them now. The good news is, now I don't have to.

**UPDATE:** How do you think my message went over? To deaf ears. More saber rattling, more demands for a plan or a schedule. Okay, so I'm putting the ex in the bill pile with Wells Fargo. And I'm taking the emotion out of my response.

"Talk to the hand. You'll get it as soon as I get it. I'll let you know in real time as I know more."

# FINDING SOMETHING TO LAUGH ABOUT

"If we can laugh about it later, we can decide to laugh about it now."

I tried to keep my joy and wits about me as well.

# Team Dad, "Even When We Can No Longer Be Together"

I put on the LiveStrong wristband on Father's Day this year. I was wearing the band in honor of my father, who died over twenty years ago, and my long-time mentor, who died six months ago. That's why I put the band on. But the conversations I did have were with MY KIDS.

For both of my kids the yellow band was a piece of jewelry. Like a watch or another colorful band. Both of them kinda knew who Lance Armstrong was. Neither had ever heard of LiveStrong or knew what the wristband was about. But as a TEAM, we wore the bands for our own reasons. I can see how binding up your positive energy with other cancer survivors or families of cancer survivors is a powerful support. With just the three of us, there was something magical about giving my kids these bands and having them wear them.

We talked about cancer. We talked about my dad. We talked about my friend who died. They had accompanied me to the wake at his house. And then we went swimming. And we put on lots of sunscreen.

And so the 30 days have passed with very little conversation outside my little Team Mac. And we're over halfway through the summer. And what a summer. I've been taking Fridays off to simply hang with them. Do what they want to do. Do nothing. Go to the pool, the lake, the movie, the corner convenience store to get a slurpee. And something occurred to me. I didn't really get much "hang time" with my dad.

So I am basking in these moments. Storing my own warm times and giving my kids the memory of a dad who knew how to hang and be flexible and had the strength to throw them high and far into the water. And that I think is the lesson I learned.

I let them go watch a terrible summer movie by themselves while I telecomputed from inside the mall. They wanted to go, I didn't. I really didn't. So we worked out a compromise. And the bands symbolized that bond we are establishing. Trust. Care. Togetherness even when we are apart.

And maybe that's the biggest lesson: Celebrate togetherness even when we are no longer able to be together. I feel their connection: my kids AND my father and father figures. While I am here, I will make this connected team of three the most important goal of my waking hours. And even as the yellow bands lose their charm and get put in a drawer, the memory of the throws into the cold, deep, lake water will never be lost.

# *What I Need to Tell You: Take Heart. It Gets Better.*

I am happy.

My writings and poems about desire have really become about hoping and striving towards "what's next."

I had a friend ping me on Facebook yesterday after reading one of my poems. She said, "They make me so sad for you." I was surprised. But I can understand how things might come off that way, especially if you are entering The Off Parent from one of the more emotional posts. But I want to be clear, this is a process, and the blog is large enough to contain the anger, the depression, the joy, the thrill of new relationships, and the frustration at dealing with a woman who no longer thinks I'm hot shit. (That's okay, it's mutual.) Overall, the picture I am hoping to paint... WAIT. That's not the idea. I'm not trying to put a bow around the process of divorce. Let's try again.

I would not want divorce for ANYONE. That said, my divorce has become one of the defining and re-defining moments of my life. I would not say I wanted the divorce or that it was MY idea...but... I was starting to stand up for a situation that had become unbearable for me.

The difference between my ex-wife's perspective and mine was minor. Critical, but minor. In the large scheme of things, I was also demanding a change.

MY PERSPECTIVE: This demand was the only way I had to effect change from within my marriage. I was arguing and demanding answers to some dark questions from the perspective that I WANTED THE MARRIAGE TO CONTINUE.

HER PERSPECTIVE: (somewhat paraphrased, but we went over it a number of times in therapy, so I'm not putting words into her mouth) She was unhappy with the marriage and saw no signs of things changing or getting better; thus it was better for her to move to something different.

The points of leverage changed dramatically when she let me know, in therapy, that she had consulted an attorney. I was crushed and panicked but unsurprised. The anger she had been demonstrating in action and words over the previous 12 months had all but wrecked my positive outlook. This admission was only revealed by my direct ask: "Have you already been to see a lawyer?" When she said yes, I just about hit the eject button right there. I did the sober thing and expressed my dismay in a rational manner and left the session feeling absolutely lost about what to do next.

In the process of the next few days, primarily via email, I ranted and demanded she make a decision. She demurred and deflected for a couple of days. But in the end, she asked me to leave the house and give her some space, some relief from the stress and tension she and the kids were experiencing. Um, what?

In the end, I refused. It was March. My line was, "The process of divorce takes time. There is no hurry. And I'm not going to throw my kid's lives into this hell before the school year is up. We've been living as roommates for a year, we can do it for another two months. We can split sleeping on the couch."

Somewhere in the back of my mind, in my rapidly crashing heart, I was certain she would see the error of her ways and come back. I knew, however, in my rational mind, that this was not going to happen.

A few sessions before the hammer fell, the therapist had asked a pivotal question, "How do you feel about the marriage and this process at this point?"

I went first. "Hopeful."

Her word was "Cynical."

Fuck.

I think that was the beginning of my revelation into the darkness that now separated the two of us. It was different for each of us. But the pain, sadness, and anger were just as potent for each of us. I like to think I was on the optimist side of the whole deal, but I was pretty disheartened.

All that said… as water under the bridge…

Today, nine years later, I am happy. Alone. But happy. And I try my best not to pass judgment on her and her new husband, who has given her strength and steadiness. My daughter says she likes him. That's enough for me.

As I cursed, raged, pleaded, and cried at my wife trying to get her to come back to the marriage, I was also certain that I could not do it alone. Two people have to be IN for a marriage to work. So she exited before me. Probably, maybe, that whole year of blinding anger was really her way of trying to help ME exit. But I'm projecting now.

When the agreement was made to divorce, I also demanded the right to stay in the house until the kids were out of school. A shitty-hard decision, but I did not want to re-enact the gross and bitter divorce struggle of my parents. It was my argument, even against the therapist, that remaining in the house while the kids finished their school year at elementary school was much better than me leaving the house immediately.

Take heart. It gets better.

And today, I would assure you that my kids are thriving. And while the ex and I don't communicate much, we have kids who love both of us and are seeing how we can still care about each other while moving in new directions with our lives.

So as I write poems about being "a poet rather than a player," I mean to be happy about it. This journey has taken some amazingly wonderful turns. And the next one is coming right up.

# Creative Parenting and the Gifts of Enthusiastic Participation

The ex used to criticize me for how much I liked to play with the kids as opposed to disciplining and enforcing rules with them. (I think this is a very common husband–wife issue.) She would want the family to do chores, and I'd be out back chasing them around the yard or playing tickle tag on the bed, completely messing the house up.

Maybe men and women have different styles. The dad is the one who's supposed to rough-house. The mom is the one who's supposed to offer comfort and tenderness. The dad is the one who's supposed to play games, incite rule-breaking, and ignore curfews. The mom is the one who has to slog away in the kitchen until the dishes are done and the counters are all spotless.

BUT…I'm here to tell you, it doesn't have to be this way. And I think my ex could have had a profound effect on the kids had she spent more time in high-energy play than as angry-energy chore-master.

Let's see how things have turned out so far.

My kids have never wondered about how much I loved them. I was usually there wrestling and hugging and soothing the bumps that come from falling off the bed the 15th time. We have a physical closeness that still draws them to jump in the "big bed" when they stay over at my house. WIN.

Although my musical pursuits have never paid off financially, both my kids love music and they both play an instrument. My son at 12 got a middle-school award for his orchestra enthusiasm. WIN.

Gaming and other flights of imagination. My son became the ringleader of a small band of Minecraft kids from his school. Essentially they quest together, with my son playing the narrator role (like dungeon master in D&D).

And while my kitchen sink is still often filled with dishes (how did I buy a house without a dishwasher again?), my kids are clean, happy, and on time for school and other events. And there is ZERO nagging or complaining about chores or homework. It's a very different place here at my house than the days when I was parenting with the ex.

Perhaps some of it comes down to the core approach to relationships. In an early example, I recall my then-wife demanding of my second grader daughter, "If you don't get your homework done, right now, there will be no TV." My daughter burst into tears. As I joined the scene, I asked, "Hey honey, how's your homework going? Is there anything I can help you with?"

One approach was authoritarian and matter of fact but lacked any compassion or connectivity with the child. My approach was to join with my daughter and see what she needed to get her work done.

My kids are continuing to thrive after the divorce. And I give credit to my ex for working hard to keep our friction out of our kids' lives. But she treats me in the same way she commanded my daughter: "Where's the money you owe me? How much can you pay? When can you pay it? Oh, and by the way, I'm sorry you're having trouble." I guess it's the way she was raised.

My kids have been raised to expect a warm and joining approach to school work, problems, and aspirations. I'm always on their side. And they have been given an example of a life filled with enthusiastic play and love of playing music. I think those are transferable skills that will continue to serve them throughout their lives. And I couldn't be happier with that picture.

## *More Play Summer*

The concept that we learn most of our relationship patterns from our family of origin is fairly well documented. What we learn from Mom and Dad is either (1) what we want to do or (2) what we don't want to do. Often we are not clear on pulling the two different concepts apart. And more often, the connections are obscured by emotion or lifelong baggage.

Today, I had a moment of realization about my family of origin and the disastrous path my dad and mom took.

I walked down to the lake from my modest house. And the sign above reminded me, "Oh yeah, this needs to be a play more summer." And I thought about my parents and our monstrous house on the lake. While my dad was successful in business, his relationship skills were limited and eventually destroyed by alcoholism. And what I missed, once my father moved out of the house (I was five) was the time and space to play with and really get to know my dad. Or, more importantly, know that he loved me. Somewhere deep in my heart, I'm still not sure of that one.

My dad worked hard every day, and as part of his come-down each night, he would have a few toddies with the boys in the office next door. His success was limitless. His medical practice was thriving. He had just completed a stunning lake house and would drive his boat to the country club in the mornings and drive his car from there to work. It was a golden life. Well, you would think it should be.

But my dad was really mad about something. He was always mad. [Hmmm. This sounds a bit too familiar.] The anger of my father is legendary even among my friends. He was an ass all the time. And somehow he resented his own success, because he had to keep working so hard to maintain it.

My mom said she made a proposition to my father one time early on, as the success was coming but the stress was also growing with it. She offered to go with him, anywhere, take some time to enjoy the money he'd been making, get away from it all. He declined.

And in the real sense of the word, he declined from there, even as his financial success shot upward.

By the time my mom gave him the ultimatum, the drink or her and the kids, he was probably too far down his own destructive path to imagine that recovery was possible. And being a doctor, AA was out of the question. He insisted to me, years later, as I was a son pleading with him to get help for his drinking, "I don't have a problem."

Today, swimming in the lake by myself, I was noticing my life at this moment. While I'm struggling a bit financially, I'm sure that I will continue to pull up from the strained economy. And even as my kids are traveling on a summer vacation with my ex and her boyfriend, I am happy.

What I have, however, that is so different from my father, is a clear and loving relationship with both my daughter and my son. They KNOW how much I love them. They will never wonder if they are enough. I tell them all the time.

And I have made some choices to keep this clarity of purpose at the forefront of my life. I could work more. I could go back to Dell and slave it out at the corporate level again. But in those two years, even as my life was following the life dream of many, I was unhappy. It was almost enough to keep me there. I loved coming home to my wife and kids in the affluent neighborhood and knowing that I had provided for their well-being and support. But there was an imbalance.

My dad got on a trajectory of success and big money that would've been very hard to get off. My exit was easier. I was no longer willing to be shut out sexually from my wife, and I was also not willing to just jump into the next corporate job to make that fantasy picture come back together. It was a fantasy that was killing me, making me fat, separating me from time with my kids. I made a choice.

Today, swimming in a modest public park, I recognized the pressure my father must've been under, and I said a little prayer that I learned from his early death, that possessions and wealth don't bring you joy. In the end, the pressure of those things may be what separates you from the most important things in your life, your family.

My father lost his family in his divorce. But he made choices to go down (and stay on) the alcoholic path. I have not made the same choices. And my hope is that my ex-wife will find some joy in life, some relief from the constant anger aimed at me. I am certain I was not my father's issue...in the same way I am certain I was not my ex's anger problem, either.

We each have to grow and evolve as individuals. We have no choice. I think I have evolved into a more caring and more dedicated father than my father could be. And today in the lake, I gave thanks to my health, love, and awareness.

More. Play. Summer.

# A Moment of Zen With the Ex-Wife

The disconnects with the ex are humorous sometimes. More so now that we are not married. While we were married, the disconnect could lead to months of shunning from the one I love. But some points of contact or conflict can provide funny insights into the workings of her mind and maybe continued contempt for me. ("If we can laugh about it later, we can laugh about it now.")

First up is the continuous process of checking-in on the nights the kids are with the other parent. For my son, who has a phone and is almost always on Skype when he's awake and not at school, it's easy. My daughter is a bit more hard to reach. So often I'm left to text the ex, asking for her to call me. And here's the common response. (At least once a week she fails to deliver the message in time for me to get a phone call from my daughter.)

May 19, 2013, 7:46 PM

**Can c call me?**

Sent as Text Message

May 19, 2013, 8:12 PM

**Sorry just seeng this - she should be calling you now**

I can assure you that when she is not with her boyfriend she is watching the texts. I've seen her at all kinds of events glued, laughing, and texting someone. So the idea that text on her phone didn't light up her synapses...very unlikely. But of course, this example is only 30 minutes. The response time varies greatly. Often I will ask for a call by say 7:00 p.m. and won't ever get a pingback or a call from my daughter. She always responds the next day with, "I'm sorry." But it's a pretty shitty passive-aggressive move to prevent your kids from talking to the other parent. Get your business out of our business, won't you?

But a really funny moment happened yesterday. Here's the email I got in the morning.

Are you missing a pair of glasses?

Sent from my iPhone

I checked my spots and sure enough, one of my two pairs of glasses was missing. We confirmed the color and yes, I had somehow dropped them at her house. She followed up with a question about how they might have ended up at the foot of her bed.

> "Oh, i'm sorry, i spent a minute petting E [our dog], they must've been in my breast pocket. I love that dog. I try to give her a pat every time I'm in your house, I hope that's okay. I'm not trying to be snooping or invasive, and she's usually asleep in your bed. (oops)"

Whew! That could've been an odd moment. And here's what happened next.

She said it was awkward because she had to ask her boyfriend if they were his. Huh? So of the two pair of glasses I had while we were married, you didn't recognize one of the pair? Wow. Yes, that would be an awkward question to ask your boyfriend, but even more odd that you'd have to ask your husband of 10 years. I think.

And in typical fashion, she pulled a fuck you in the transaction. She said she was leaving them on the kitchen counter for me to pick up. When the kids and I dropped by a few hours later, they were nowhere to be found. I texted her.

So maybe she's just forgetful. Maybe she's busy. Maybe she's discombobulated. But she's also being a jerk. Is it passive aggressive-ness or just plain assholeness? I can't decide.

I'm not looking to keep a tight leash on her or my kids. But I don't block them from getting in touch with her; in fact, I facilitate it. Oh well, we're different animals with different styles.

I kinda like the response, "Damn yes sorry." I might have to try that out. What I can tell you is I am not waiting for her to change and be a different person. I did that for way too long. I'm a learning individual. I won't be trying to change someone or waiting for her to get a clue. Next time, this very next time, I'm gonna nip that impulse in me before it starts.

# THINGS BEGIN AGAIN - FALLING APART

My divorce was finalized in August 2010, and my next full-time job came along in December of that year. I appeared to land on my feet at a fairly high-profile and well-paying gig. Immediately I started looking for a place to live. I knew with the way credit works that I needed to establish myself as a homeowner as quickly as possible. In February I found a smallish house in a neighborhood a lot less expensive than our family home but within my kids' school district. In March we launched the "gnome house" chapter of our lives. My kids were in fourth and sixth grade at the time, and my house was actually closer to my son's middle school than their mom's home. It was a short-lived victory.

In July of that first year, my employer changed the entire business model and eliminated my position after six months. Now, I could give into my mom and sister's evaluation that I jumped too early, but I knew that my options for buying were going to be much harder without the big job. I was glad I had a home, but I collapsed into a summer of hardship as I struggled to find work again. At the same time, my kids and I had a great summer. We swam in the nearby lake. We played basketball and soccer in the twilight of the summer evenings, when the Texas heat gave way. We had an adventure together. And for all intents and purposes we were happy in our little house. On the days (most of them) when they were not with me,

I thrashed and struggled with my life and the impending loss of my newly established home.

When school started up again, things began to fall apart for me.

# Gone. A Pause at Summer's End

And out of the clear blue sky, it is gone, and I am sad.

It's been a great summer. Through many challenges and growth opportunities, but we made it. And with the school drop-off today, after a three-day weekend, I find myself struggling to maintain momentum. I've got plenty of work to do, so it's not lack of requirements. It's something else.

Little reminders of the loss of my children sometimes sneak up on me when I'm not paying attention. And the coffee doesn't stave off the bummed-out feelings. The nap that sounds like an escape is really just temporary sedation.

In divorce you lose everything.

Maybe this is preparation for the empty nest that's at least five years away. Or this is just part of being a single parent with less than half-time custody. But I'm not sure it's about custody, or schedules, or even the divorce. I think it's me. My sadness. My losses. The grip of my daughter's hand as we walk into Starbucks for her lunch sandwich. Those things that we take for granted, the ever-present child, is stolen away by the changes required by divorce.

And as always, it is a growth opportunity to me. It is a moment to pause and reflect. Remember not to fall into soulful revery and sadness. And pick up with the work to be done. But the pause IS important.

This is what we've lost.

And with so much to gain from the newly available time, the nights and weekends "off," the opportunities to find what makes us GO again, there are still these little pauses, setbacks, to remember our own pain. And to walk on into what's next.

This is not about them. It's not about her. It's about me.

The journey is long. And, for the most part, we travel alone. We have choices about how we move and grow with the changes, losses, and new wins in our lives.

Time for a walk in the sun. The work will get done. The days will grow shorter. And another chapter is waiting to be created.

# Check Engine Light: How Long Until a Breakdown Forces Repairs?

The summer is done, the kids are clicking right along in their new classes, and even my work seems to be okay. But the "service engine soon" light keeps coming on. And it's more than a metaphor. While I am on the positive side of the divorce, and growing stronger by the minute, some of my fundamentals are still damaged.

**First fail:** I am not making enough money. I'm behind on my mortgage, trying to avoid bankruptcy through additional work, and applying for full-time jobs. And the work is coming. Two new clients and a former client are all asking for more hours. That's good, but it's still "coming."

**Second fail:** I'm still not doing a very good job of keeping the dishes done or the house picked up. It's easy to let things go a bit when there's no one to entertain (I even used this as a way to keep me from pursuing a sexual relationship, last month). But I'm not doing the greatest job of setting an example for my kids. I can do better.

**Third fail:** Inspection and registration stickers are both expired on my car. And I have a ticket out there waiting for me. That damn "service engine soon" light means something is wrong, something that will prevent them from giving me a healthy inspection sticker until it's fixed. Sure this is how the system is supposed to work, but … GRRR.

So at what point does the system (me) simply break down?

There was a moment, during the darkest part of my marriage, when my then-wife said to me, "There is no rescue coming. We are it. There is nobody else." At that moment we were still in the collaborative mode of fighting against the economic struggles caused by 9-11 and my subsequent depression, which brought my earning power, as a consultant, down in a hurry.

Is there a reset button? What's the reset for me? Fall apart again?

In fact, even as I face the most difficult financial time of my life, where my back is pressed against the proverbial wall, I'm feeling stronger than ever. October has begun, healthcare might be more affordable for me and my family, and I'm ramping up towards my birthday in November, when my powers of strength and imagination tend to peak.

The breakdown happened in my marriage. The continued breakdowns were facilitated by our relationship that began to spin out of control at some point. And while the financial fight before me is high, I raise my cup of coffee every morning at 6:00 a.m. and laugh at the day. I am alive. I am happy. I am thriving. And I WILL FIX THE CAR, when I have the cash.

# Losing Touch in the Off Times

And as the long holiday without the kids continues into this week, I am trying to remain relevant in their lives. Last night, when we video conferenced on a mobile phone, I was amazed by by how different they appeared to me. I don't want to be a footnote in their lives, I want to be a main cast member.

I am aware just how far the distance can be. So much of their daily lives, their school routines, their haircuts and clothing choices seem so mundane, and yet I regret missing out on every single one. And for a second, looking at them on this video call, I became aware of how different I also might appear to them. How alien and distant after four or five days have passed. This dad in a box, snuggled with a kitty, reaching out for my five or 10 minutes of connection through a video conference.

I felt the first pangs of Divorcemas heading in. Just what I was working to avoid. And sometimes it rushes up to greet you. A loop. A moment that catches you off guard and you're bummed. WHAT?

Just noticing this is enough for now. I've got my kids this weekend for a refresh and reconnect. But I'm aware of a tenderness that I experienced. And of course the energy and rise I've been on couldn't be sustained forever. So a bit of coasting, slowing down, and paying attention to the basics again.

As the cold fronts are hitting all around, today. Food. Exercise. Sleep. And enjoying my kids while they are here.

# Winning the Battle, Losing the War

She's ready to turn my month-and-a-half-late ass over to the Attorney General's office. She let me know yesterday via email. And as I was responding via email, I think I identified and called out the crux of the issue.

Perhaps this can provide some illumination into my thinking. It's not that I'm late, it's not that she needs this money right this second. It seems to be the "principle of the thing." And what I understood while writing this message to her was how closely this situation echoes much of the trouble in our relationship. These actions closely resemble the actions and misunderstandings that led to the divorce.

I don't think it's about the money. I don't think it's about her fears that I won't ever pay or get caught up. (I've never failed before.) I think it's about having someone to focus your anger on. Whatever is wrong with her world, I am still at the center of her problems. Now, I don't believe this. I didn't believe it in the closing moments of our relationship. As I asked her, "Do you think you are suddenly going to be a happy person when I walk out the door?" She didn't GET HAPPY.

And she's still unhappy with me. And of course, I am to blame for her unhappiness, because she's owed this money, and she might never see it, and… WAIT. In what universe? Like I've got an option to bolt on my child support? NO.

So if it's not the child support, really. Well, I think it's easier to see from here. Let me know if I've got something wrong. I'm prepared to hear that my logic and emotional truth is OFF on this one. But it felt so right when I wrote it, that I knew I had to continue the drama from yesterday.

And with this letter, I'm setting in action the process that will remove "money" and "timing" and "enforcement" from our vocabulary.

+++

*Dear ___,*

*I am certain that I don't know your situation. And I'm not sure it has any bearing on my options.*

*I did not run out of money. And I am not trying to keep you in the dark about my situation. My company shifted to NET 15 on me. Instantly changing my cash flow. And, of course things happen (car repair, computer loss) that can compound the situation. That's all that has changed on my end. A couple new clients in the pipe for both my company and me personally SHOULD open things up again.*

*Your responses to the information I have been able to give you is, "That's not good enough."*

*And yesterday you basically said you'd rather have the AG's office sort it out for us. For the next eight years! Wow.*

*So that's what you're gonna get. It's fucked. And there is no way to unplug once we've entered the system.*

*Therefore, my responsible duty is to recalculate what you are owed, what you got in credit based on my projected income. I'm guessing it's a bit more than half, averaged-out since we've been divorced. So you can re-run all your calculations based on that idea and see where you end up.*

*My preferred approach was to honor the expectation, even as it affected me quite adversely. In the name of being nice, giving you everything I hoped to give you, that is what I was trying to communicate to you.*

*But it feels like some macabre redo of our divorce. Me asking, "Are you sure this is what you want?"*

*Want to calculate the money based on reality? Want to bring the AG in to help you?*

*Done! And done!*

*My "thank you" response yesterday was genuine. You are forcing me (again) to look at an unhealthy relationship. I am being given an opportunity to clean up my own shit. And, with the help of the state, I will gladly disconnect from the cash flow crisis mode one of us seems to benefit from.*

*I hope this process will allow us to remain friendly and cordial with our co-parenting. All of us benefit from being flexible. Unfortunately, I'm pretty sure the AG's process is setup to fight against flexibility. And maybe it will help us keep our business to parenting.*

*You will now be able to call your case worker and explore "collection" and "enforcement" options with them. Hope that serves you.*

# *Me, Deadbeat Dad? Um…*

I cannot seem to get a handle on the triggers for the ex's money demands. I know they often happen on Sunday nights. Perhaps she's paying bills, or just planning for the week ahead, and up comes the check box, GET MORE MONEY.

I understand. I understand all too well. But… This message from her, in a typical escalation of demands involving the words "collections" and "attorney":

"The frame is that we have to pay kids expenses before we cover our houses and cars and bills. I am paying my part. I won't sell this house to pay your part while you take the stance that your child support stands in line behind Wells Fargo."

Um, it's actually backwards in my book. Of course she's not struggling to meet Wells Fargo's demands, she's talking about the incidentals, the nice to haves, the keeping up with the standard of living we have come to expect. And thus our kids have come to expect.

Hello! The facts are clear. And I stated them when she first demanded a divorce. "We can hardly afford one house in this neighborhood, do you think we're going to be able to afford two?"

Of course, the truth is, she didn't. She expected SHE would be able to stay in the beautiful house in the beautiful neighborhood with greenbelts and tennis courts. She didn't care too much about what I was going to do. She still doesn't.

But the reality is we cover our housing and food needs before the incidentals.

Another thing she doesn't seem to factor in, she's got zero debt (I took the credit card debt) and she's got in excess of $30k in retirement funds (much of it paid in while I was the one bringing in the excess income that afforded our 100% contribution) AND she has the house that easily has $60k in equity after costs.

She was going to sell it. At the end of last year. She decided not to, claiming it was easier not to have to gamble on our daughter being transfered to a different elementary school. Probably the move could've been averted with a petition to the school board.

For whatever reason (maybe she's going to get married soon and they want to get a house together), she's decided that she's done "affording" the kids what they need because I can't pay.

I keep saying, "It's a delay, not a default." But she doesn't want to hear it. She doesn't have to hear it. And she doesn't care.

I guess in the eyes of the law, I am in default, I am a deadbeat dad who is two months behind on his child support. And when she rattles the Attorney General's office or the threat of lawyering up, I laugh. I can't do anything else.

"You are in default on child support. It's your responsibility to give ideas and plans for how to cover your part of their expenses. You can't opt-out of supporting your kids, and telling me you won't tell me any information about support moving forward is opting out. "

What I keep trying to say is:

"Whatever. You're escalating again. My frame is we pay for shelter and food then other stuff. I've given you every bit of information I have. If that is defaulting to you, so be it. I am delayed in my ability to pay. That's quite different than defaulting or you needing to hire help to 'collect.' All I can give you, still, is an agreement to pay 100% of my share and a willingness to give you all information as I have it."

It's never enough. In fact, in our marriage, it was never enough. She's not going to be happy with me even if I was paying extra. But she's happy to point the dagger at me and threaten me. She doesn't have to be nice.

But am I a deadbeat dad? Am I failing my kids?

Maybe so, if you consider that child support of a woman in an affluent neighborhood in a nice house without debt should be paid before my mortgage company and electric bill. I guess without a house I could go live with my sister again. But the only relief selling my house would bring is about two months of catch up. What about the next eight years?

I'm not aware that this pattern is something that is very familiar to me. **Women giving up on me.**

I won't stand for it. I cannot pay her incidentals (summer camps, new shoes, fancy clothes) before I pay for my own shelter. I've never indicated that I would not catch up. But I am also not responsible for her cash flow issues.

She wants to plan a trip to Washington, DC with the kids. Great. She wants to buy plane tickets in advance. Great.

I want to keep my house, keep the lights on, and occasionally be able to take a date to dinner.

Here's what I have to keep repeating: "I am making enough money to catch up over the summer on everything."

Beyond that, it's drama and escalation. There's no reason I have to buy into that and no reason I should start feeling bad about myself and my deadbeat approach to a difficult situation.

# *Stinging the Hand that Feeds*

Just days ago the ex and I were exchanging ideas around me catching up on my child support payments. (I'm a bit more than a month behind.) She continued to use phrases like "enforcement" and "collection," but I was certain she was saber rattling. Until today when she basically gave me the option to turn our process over the the Attorney General's office, or she would start the process without me.

So much for working it out between us.

Here's the sting. Our divorce decree was based on an expected income that greatly exceeds the amount of money I've actually brought in since the divorce. The result of her actions will now cause me to reset the child support payments based on my actual income. Rather than smooth out her "payments," she most likely will get less than I was planning on paying.

And, in fact, she's forcing the issue, in the same way she forced the divorce. But rather than be angry, as I was when I first got her ultimate escalation email, I am now feeling some relief. I sent her a follow-up email, after my "are you sure this is what you want?" email. In the second email, I said thank you. Again. It is like a replay of the divorce.

But even this is going to be a good thing.

1.  I need to clean up my shit, financially.
2.  We can take the "we" process out of the money.
3.  I will likely get a payment schedule that is more in line with

what I'm actually making.

So a full reset. Steps along the path.

She said something kind of funny at the end of her flaming fuck you email.

"This is a tough patch but we always seem to work through things."

Um. Yes we do, of course. There's not a lot of choices, for the next eight years. So now the courts will be my keeper. Oh boy. It's a bit like our marriage. For some reason she did not believe me. Or she has merely grown tired of dealing with me. Again.

# Reassessing the Deadbeat Dad vs. Good Guy Dad

[Note of self observation: I'm feeling really sad now, at having written this. It cuts back to the leftover hurt of the relationship and my own wish that we could've afforded for my kids to have a stay-at-home mom. But we couldn't manage that dream if we wanted to live in our neighborhood and send our kids to the good schools. So here we are. And now, giving her less money feels good to me but also re-scuffs the hurt of losing our dream together. But that, of course, cannot be recovered.]

Okay the process was a long time coming.

**FIRST:** The primary online response (100% women) to my blog was "pay her what you owe her." In fact, one woman went on to tell me she imagined my observations about my divorce were not how she saw things. (Um, duh! And thanks...) What I heard was a lot of anger about dads not paying their child support. And an immediate vilification of the man, even me, who appears to be making excuses. I'm guessing that's what my ex-wife thinks as well. That I'm making excuses. But that's not the reality of the situation. Not by far.

**SECOND:** When pushed to the state as guardian model of management, I felt an immediate relief. Never again would my ex-wife be allowed to pelt me with the "when can I expect the money" emails and texts. Once the Attorney General's office is involved, I can simply refer her to her caseworker. Sounds kind of hard ass, but that's how it feels to me, too. Getting my good will tossed back to the lawyers, or in this case, the legal machine of the great state of Texas.

**THIRD:** The kicker in the process is this: I have been OVERPAYING. I was aware I was OVERPAYING. I was willing to keep OVERPAYING in "anticipation" of returning to my previous corporate high of earning. So now, rather than OVERPAY any more, I'm going to reset the numbers and will start paying the actual awarded percentage of my income to my ex-wife (approximately 20% before taxes).

So my monthly bill payments are going to go down significantly with this reset as well. Hell, I'm starting to feel kind of chipper about the whole thing.

In my mind I was trying to be the good dad. I was anticipating the income that hadn't turned up yet. I WAS/AM working my ass off to get there again. And in a moment of impatience and impulsive anger, she set me off to re-evaluate the entire situation.

I warned her that I would do this. And I did my dog-like grovel, "Are you sure this is what you want?" JUST LIKE IN THE CLOSE OF OUR MARRIAGE.

Today I sent her the response, updating her with my PLAN. Just an FYI, "Here's my unofficial estimate."

I walk into this Memorial Day weekend, a long weekend WITH my kids, with a sense of relief. I'm not sure what she's feeling now, but that's not my problem. And I could be wrong. Maybe the accountant will add things up differently. Maybe I made a lot more money than I thought I did. I don't think so, but maybe…

Set the machine in motion, and I'm gonna get a refund in the form of no-payments until we're caught up. And then I'm guessing my actual payments, based on reality rather than good-guy math, will sober her ass up pretty quickly. Again, not my issue. But you can almost see the grin on my face, right?

Now, I'm guessing, this post will cause another round of women being mad with me at being an asshole. What I thought I was doing in being the good guy dad was to provide for my kids and ex-wife in the way they had been accustomed to living. Unfortunately, that didn't account for the economic recovery. And of course, SHE didn't have too much concern for MY LIVING CONDITIONS. So being 45 days behind is going to turn into the equivalent of winning a small lottery prize.

Again, I'm sorry for the anger this kind of negotiation and settlement causes people. And I'm sorry there are real deadbeat dads who have no intention of ever paying what they are supposed to pay their children and ex-wife. But that's not me. I'm ready to get things back to the REAL picture. She really liked working the spreadsheets. I guess this is information she's going to have to re-calculate. And now I can do the same.

And now I can pick my head back up off the ground for feeling so beat up and trying to manage an unmanageable expense. Heck, maybe never having to be harassed about money by my ex-wife will be a good thing, too. It's not personal, right? It's just business.

# I Must Be Insane: It's the End of the World, and I Feel Fine

There's not much that is going to plan at this moment. YET, I'm happily plugging along on my path and flipping the bird to the ex-wife, bill collectors, family members who think they know exactly what I need to do. Fuck 'em.

And as I checked in with my therapist this morning, he said, "Either you've gone completely insane, or everyone else has." I'm gonna stick with our assumption that unhealthy systems don't like for people to get healthy or stand up against them.

Let me be clear, **I am behind on my child support payments.** THIS I KNOW. But I am not avoiding them or trying to hide behind excuses. It's pretty simple. A client's business took a hit recently and changed their payment terms with me. I'm not working any less or taking time off, but I'm not getting paid with the same frequency. They will get caught up, too. And when they do, I will give my ex and my kids all the money they deserve. This is not a choice I am making to stiff them or to begin my slip towards becoming a deadbeat dad.

Of course, that does not help my ex and her own cash flow problems. I tried to have a discussion with her, since she keeps sending messages of some urgency. Here's how the conversation went.

ME: I'm happy to meet or talk at anytime this week, if you'd like to talk about things.
HER: First question: When can you pay me?

ME: Um. I'm not sure.
HER: Next question: How much?
ME: Okay, I see this is how the conversation would go if we were to get together. Maybe that's not necessary. Let me ask a question. "Is there some extenuating circumstance or something I'm missing that is causing our kids great suffering? Or is it just cash flow?"
HER: I am incurring debt because of things you are not paying for.

Ah, so... It's really just a choice, then, to pound me for the money, even when I've been as clear as possible about my financial situation. Am I going on vacations or spending money on anything other than food and shelter? NO. And I won't rehash how her financial situation is just fine... Not my business or my concern.

You see, knowing that you owe taxes is not the same as having the money to pay them. Avoiding penalties is great if you have the money. When you dial back to survival mode you have to thicken your skin a bit, and take care of what you CAN take care of and ignore the rest of the URGENT MESSAGES that come from everyone looking for their money.

I tried to explain this to my ex. Her urgency didn't translate for me. In fact, it just made me a bit more frustrated as I tried to give her information (she was asking for information) but no firm dates and amounts. That's what she wants. How much and when. That's fine. But it's not possible for me to answer that question. And there's a wrinkle that I'm looking into as well. (Based on actual income vs. estimated income, I've overpaid her significantly since we got divorced.)

As we move along, perhaps the urgency or villainy will be moved from me to someone or something else for her. Today I'm her target, but I'm getting ready to punch back. Or not. Just like my divorce recovery class says, "Treat them like a convenience store clerk. Just take care of business and get out."

When she came by on Saturday to pick up the kids, she looked great. She's still my type. I could see how I would still find her attractive and want to date her. I would hope, today, that my self-awareness would allow me see some of the fatal flaws before falling in love with her. I noticed her and her attractiveness like I might a pretty waitress, and then we conducted the business of transferring the kids' stuff.

I wish her well. The better she does, the better my kids do when they are with her. And I hope her boyfriend turns out to be more reliable and a better honey-do than I was.

I will get her all of her money. All of the money that belongs to my kids. At this moment, that money is for extracurricular things. And I don't have a single extracurricular dollar. That's why the downstairs bathroom is in need of repairs. And why the creditors, including her, will have to wait until things move back into the plus column. They've been heading in the right direction all summer, but a few hitches along the way, and I'm still plugging along in survival mode.

The good news is: even under the duress of the financial and familial stress, I am still centered in my own happiness. That is the only happiness I can manage.

# SOLDIERING ALONG AS CO-PARENTS

We struggled on. I continued to profess my intention of getting caught back up with the child support that was set during the divorce at my "big corporate job" rate. She started feeling the pressure of the cash call as well, and there is no blame here. She was a very responsible money manager. In her mind she was doing what she felt was necessary. I was doing what I thought was necessary as well. I remember an email exchange between us where she said, "You seem to think that your mortgage and expenses are more important than your responsibility to your children. I don't understand that."

Um… My response was this: "I think we knew this was going to be hard. And I think Dad deserves a place to live and a food and electricity to provide a place for himself and his kids, when he has them. I will get caught up on the child support, and I assure you I am not spending any discretionary money. I have no discretionary money. I am working to find a job so I can keep my house and resume full payments to you."

At this point I was just irregular. When things got really bad is when I actually missed a full payment. Her emails became more hostile. And our "conversations" devolved into sometime resembling this exchange. ME: "I think we should talk about the kids' summer plans." HER: "When will you have the next payment?" ME: "Um… I don't know. I have some prospects, but nothing has come through." HER:

Silence. And that's how the communications between us, that had been positive and kid-focused, got off track. And things went downhill fast after she started refusing to discuss anything with me that didn't involve a payment date and plan from me.

# Tell Me Again Why You Think This Is a Good Idea?

So you sued me. Um… For the last six months, you won't talk to me, other than texts and emails. Okay. I think it's a terrible idea, but okay.

Money has never been easy to talk about for me and the ex. And the awful realization, probably for both of us, is even in divorce we are strapped in the same financial boat together, for the duration of our kids' youth. Ack. It doesn't have to be terrible, or adversarial, and it didn't start out that way, until this summer.

The economy…yadda yadda. My primary contract hit a snag in April, and my income was cut in half. I have been working in a number of ways to replace that gap since, even applying for full-time gigs and giving up my ongoing business development. Everything is on the table. I'm scrambling.

When we defined our agreement, I was anticipating a quick hire by a company that was "working up an offer" for approximately $80K per year (great money if you can get it). The contract didn't go through, but my divorce did, and I agreed to child support payments in the amount that would be in line with that income level. The problem is, I have not yet achieved that income level since, at least not for more than six months at a time.

Okay, so, as things are getting REALLY tight, I let the ex know that I was going to get behind, but that I was going to keep her informed of my income and potential to pay as soon as I had the information. This did not go over well.

I understand.

She too has bills to pay, and her projections were based on counting on my support. I was apologetic, but I didn't have an answer to her question. The questions she began to hammer home week after week: "When?" and "How much?"

So I was sliding, unwillingly, down the slippery slope towards becoming a deadbeat dad. The reality was that our two household family unit required more money than when we were married, and she was as dependant on my job as she had been when we were married. The fact that she was still living in the very nice house in the very nice neighborhood was a bit of a sore subject, but I wanted what was best for my kids. And uprooting them during the divorce was not an option that either the ex or I considered reasonable.

A few years later, however, the kids are older, well-adapted to the divorce routine, and she is sitting on a house that is nearly double what mine is worth, in today's hot market. So she's got that as an option. But let's go back to the early summer.

As the first month behind wore on, my ex's patience also began to fray. Her emails became more accusatory and demanding. I even started taking them into my talky therapist to see if he could help me parse out the anger from the request. With his help I tried to craft week-after-week reasonable responses to her requests. The demand for payment or an exact payment schedule was not something I could meet. And I kept looking for work.

During the second month (again I am behind, it is my fault), she began to rattle a different saber at me. She started mentioning the Attorney General's office. As in "maybe it would be best just to turn the whole thing over to the AG's office and you can sort it out with them."

My initial reaction was disbelief. I was not hiding anything from her. In fact, my talky therapist and I agreed that giving her a weekly update would alleviate some of her anxiety and stress. We were wrong. She wanted her money and now was prepared to turn me over to the state.

At this point I took my first defensive posture of the entire process. I told her, "If you do this, I will want to go back and review what our decree said and how much I was agreeing to pay you, and reset that amount based on what I actually made." But I was asking her not to take such an adversarial position, I was trying to give her information and updates, but I could not agree to a timeline and budget that I had no idea how I could project or meet.

She pressed on and said she's going to file. I did a rough (and very conservative) review of what I had actually made in three years and that initial $80K per year estimate that my child support was calculated on. I sent her my back-of-the-napkin calculations showing I had over-paid her $16K over three years. Again, I asked her to reconsider filing against me with the state. I was happy to give her all the information I had.

She took my calculation and plea as a threat. Again, never once, did I dispute the amount she was owed or say that I was not going to pay all of it, when I had the means. But at this point I had missed a mortgage payment as well and was taking action to try to prevent losing my house.

In a seminal email in August, one day before my house was to be foreclosed on, she asked, "Any update on your house?" It seemed like a caring question. I reported back that Wells Fargo had given me another 30 days to provide additional proof of income. Five minutes later her reply came.

"I know this is bad timing for you, but I filed with the AG's office, today."

# Can Things Get Worse? Yes, Easy!

My email to her was short and... Well, it was short and with as little vitriol as I could manage. I edited for clarity. Essentially, I told her I wished she had accepted my offer to talk before taking this action. (We have a mutual friend who actually works for the Attorney General's office.) But she hadn't, and now she was going to put us both through some unnecessary process and procedure. I tried to explain, the Attorney General's office really is a way of accounting for the payments made or not made. They had limited enforcement capacity. And I was not disagreeing with the amount owed or the fact that I owed it.

You can't extract money from a person who is filing bankruptcy. There's no money here. That's the point.

She was clear and consistent in her message, the same message I got today as the closer on a round of emails about child support and Attorney General's cluster.

"I'm not contesting that you asked for us to meet and talk. And that I said no unless we could talk about child support $. It's in our parenting plan that we use email; it was a unilateral decision on your part that you'd only talk with me about certain things face to face."

Her refrain at that point, every single time I brought up talking in person, was "How much" and "When." Seriously? That's it? That's all you have for me? That's all the care you have for planning and strategizing about our kids' future?

I'm jumping ahead and skipping the throat punch again. Sorry.

So, here I go, heading into bankruptcy trying to figure out how to keep Wells Fargo from taking my one asset, and my ex has nothing but more process and procedure to throw at me. Let me slow down and take it step-by-painful-step.

In discussing the options with my new bankruptcy attorney, who extracts his $1,000+ fee at that first meeting, it's clear we need a strategy for dealing with my ex. And let's get this straight. Not a tactic, not a way to hide the truth or tuck away some assets for protection. If she's so hopping mad at me, thinking I'm spending all her child support on strippers and blow, this should clear things up.

In that first meeting, we decided that I should ask my ex to accept a lien on a small piece of property my family still owns, thereby securing her "debt" to an asset. The plan was for me to agree to all of her financial grievances to-date, sign a document giving her first-blood on any sale of this family asset... AND for the privilege of me doing this, I could then free up some money and begin paying her child support ASAP.

I said to the attorney. "I think she'll go for that. It's a win-win for her. And we're cordial. I should be able to get that over the weekend." I left feeling like I had a plan to keep my shelter. (Back down to the base of Maslow's damn hierarchy again — Dammit.)

When I asked, via email, of course, I thought my proposition would put me back in the good-guy camp. I was agreeing to sign any accounting she had (and you can bet she had them) and begin the process of getting payments to her again. Her response floored me.

"I appreciate your kind offer. But I signed an agreement with the Attorney General's office that I would not negotiate with you about child support."

BOOM.

Ten days later, I was in the attorney's office again. Turns out, without her cooperation I don't qualify for my Chapter 13 bankruptcy.

"So what, we're going to burn the place to the ground now?" I asked.

"Not that bad," the attorney said.

So get this. I withdrew my bankruptcy filing, telling the court that I would probably be filing in the future when I get my income levels to an amount that would allow me to qualify for the plan.

GET THIS: I'm trying to file for bankruptcy literally to keep the roof over my head, to get caught back up on everyone's payments, and move forward. And I didn't qualify. WTF?

I'm not sure what the next bold moves might be from the ex. I got the letter today from the Attorney General's office that they were prepared to file a mark against my credit report showing my back payments as past due. Oh boy. I guess that'll foul up my grim options on the bankruptcy even further.

The silver lining, if there is one, is this. Wells Fargo now has to go through the process of resetting my account and restarting the foreclosure process on me again. (Boy, this is not fun.) And I have a couple of months to increase my income by about 20% or lose everything. I guess my sister's spare room is still an option if I lose my house.

Again, I can't imagine being in the reverse situation and doing anything that would damage her chances of keeping her house. I wrote that to my ex yesterday as part of the exchange that ended with her email above. She's complaining about the cost of violin private lessons and I'm talking about trying to keep a house over my head. A place, by the way, where her kids spend 33.5% of their time.

Scratching my head, all I think is she's still hoppin' mad. So mad she'd like to see me fail in the biggest way. Meanwhile, she's living in a house that was afforded by my downpayment and my corporate jobs and that is almost double the value of mine. Oh well.

You walk away from the marriage, but you can't walk away from the financial enmeshment. Like it or not, we're still dependant on the other's earning power. I've been doing everything I can to find the next opportunity for my work. And I would tell you that I'm not worried. But again, I might have delusions of grandeur. I've been work-ing on replacing this income since June.

Unless she has me arrested, going for contempt or whatever those charges might be, I think I'm safe for a few months. I think my kids and I have a place to sleep and play and be a smaller family.

**NOTE:** I was really enjoying the part where I was writing less about divorce and the ex and more about aspirations and seeking love. Ho-hum. And yes, I know, I'm the asshole man/dad who's behind on his child support. So in my assessment, the deadbeat dad is a man who is doing things to prevent his ex-wife and family from thriving. A dad-having-trouble is simply a dad who cannot afford a place to live and the court-ordered payments to his ex-wife. It might be a seman-tic distinction, but it gives me some comfort. Forgive me, but I'm try-ing.

# I Am Failing in One Critical Area of Life

And it's not my best area, money.

I was listening to two men today in some kind of mentoring conversation. I heard one of them mention the areas of life work.

Spiritual Health
Mental Health
Physical Health
Financial Health

And I was like... Uh oh.

You see, I've got a problem. It is a big problem. And perhaps one I've had my entire life.

I'm kinda crazy about money. And at the moment, while I'm feeling so solid in the first three areas of life, I'm about to go down the black hole of financial meltdown. And here's the rub. The divorce has a lot to do with it.

On Monday, I will declare Chapter 13 bankruptcy to keep Wells Fargo from foreclosing on my house. It's the only asset I have along with my car. And in the middle of this, while I try and negotiate a catch-up plan with my ex-wife, she's holding up the "sorry but it's out of my hands" card. She's turned our child support "issue" over to the Attorney General's office.

Another example of "oh, I'm sorry that didn't work out for you." She cloaked it in "I know this is not a good time for you…" The velvet has worn thin on the gloves. There's no courtesy from her. No consideration of my struggles. And I guess that's okay. She's got her own issues, her own money requirements, and my reduced income over the summer didn't help her either.

I'm not proud of my necessary intervention. But it doesn't diminish my obligation to her. And still, she says in sympathy, "I'm sorry you're having to deal with this." But she really means, "Where's my money, mf?"

The one thing she could do, to help me get the terms of the bankruptcy in a safer place, is to negotiate an agreement about the back owed child support (about $10k.) The agreement actually secures the debt with a note tied to a family asset I still have a potential claim for in a future sale. It seems like a way to validate and secure her accounting of what I owe her.

When I was talking to the financial attorney, I said, "Oh this should be easy. It's actually good for her. And we're still friendly."

Her email tonight put the relationship in starker terms.

"The document I signed when I submitted the application to have the Attorney General manage the child support process, one of the things the form said was I was forbidden to negotiate with you about anything related to child support."

Yes.

Thanks, hon. You've essentially turned us over to the state's attorney for negotiation.

Again, perhaps this is for the best. I will go another route to get my bankruptcy affairs in order. And I will remember, YET AGAIN, that I can't ask her for anything. It's just business. And in the business of things, I owe her money.

The last five times I've tried to get us together to talk about things, her response has been very simple. "About what?" All she wanted to know was, "How much can you pay me? When can you pay me?" That's it.

Maybe that's the way it needs to be. Maybe she's dealing with pressures I don't know anything about. Maybe she's just mad at me, still. Either way, she's "sorry I'm having to deal with this" AND "it's out of my hands."

I give thanks for this illumination. I may have to get the message tattooed on my arm, so I can remember what I've learned. If she needs something, she will always ask, regardless of my situation, or if it's best for the kids. When I ask for something, I'd best not count on a cooperative response.

Calm down. It's okay. I've survived this far. And even with the child support burden set at about twice what I was actually earning, I've managed to get this far. I'm not going to give my house back to the bank and go live with my mom. I'm gainfully employed. I could be MORE employed, but I'm working on that, too.

I've got three of the four areas of life pretty well in hand. And the last one, I'm struggling with a bit. But I won't let a little money trouble get me down. Things don't always work out as we planned. I'm the kind of man who gets back up, with a positive attitude, and gives it another go. Alone for now.

**Reflection:** There was a moment, during the roommate period before divorce, when I asked my then-wife, "Do you think we're going to be able to afford two houses in this neighborhood?" We'd struggled mightily, just a year prior, just to keep the one house. Of course, she would receive financial help after the divorce. What I guess I was saying, where do you think I'm going to live? And now that I'm edging towards losing my house in a neighborhood that's "further out," I know that my lament was closer to the truth than I'd like to admit. No one wants to fail. No one wants to miss a payment (car, rent, child support). The shame is present and real for me at this moment.

**Update:** I'm now in the process of petitioning the state for my bankruptcy. The good news is I didn't lose my house. The gooder news is, I'm going to get my financial house in order by the order of the court. The not so good news, my ex has filed her petition with the state's attorney general, so we'll see how that all shakes down. Fun times.

# A Fool and His Money Soon Go Separate Ways

I've shied away from the big money post before. But on my "getting healthier" walk today, I heard a song that made me sort of rethink: WTF?

Let me see if I've got this right.

When we met, my ex was living in a rental house (really living with her boyfriend at the time, but I didn't know this until later). She had a great job and seemed to be making plenty of money. (Or should I say, money didn't seem to be an issue in her life.)

At that same time, I was living in a pretty swanky condo downtown (thanks mostly to my father's estate) and working full-time at my own consulting and marketing business. (Pretty much what I'm doing now.)

When we began talking mating and offspring we both agreed on a couple of things:

1. Mom should get to spend more time in the early years with the babies.

2. Mom would probably have to work part-time, eventually, since we wanted to live in a really nice neighborhood.

3. Dad would work full-time and do whatever it takes to make #1 and #2 happen.

4.  We were in this equally, equitably.

5.  We made a great team together.

For the most part, we were growing our family to plan, when 9-11 happened and changed the world for all of us.

In our little universe, which consisted of a one-year-old son, we had some cushion. But the fall of so many of our norms was hard to recover from. (I guess I've also shied away from telling the longer story of my depression... Hmm.)

So here's what happened to me, personally.

- My long-time client transitioned all of their business to a new company the August before 9-11.

- In my rebuilding plans I had scored several new clients, both real estate developers. The day after 9-11, all of my income, 100% of it, froze. My income went to zero.

- My mental wheels began to come off about nine months in, though I did manage to land a few new clients in the new post 9-11 era.

- Finally, with the upcoming birth of my daughter becoming increasingly medically complicated, I snapped. Something broke inside of me, and I no longer assumed that things were going to be okay. I broke down.

This breakdown took the form of me turning down a very stressful but lucrative opportunity that my then-wife had helped secure. And I didn't back out very gracefully. I freaked out of it. "I can't do it. I can't give them the presentation."

Over the course of the next several years, my emotional sobriety was mixed. I had good months, good runs at work, and then I would go pop and drop back into the pit of despair. The good news is my premarital condo sold for a very nice nest egg. The bad news is, while this was taking place, we were burning through that nest egg at a pretty alarming rate.

Here's where things got a little weird. And here's where the money part of my marriage really came into question for me.

While we had agreed that Mom would get to stay at home with the kiddos as much as possible, I began to see how dependent we had become on MY income. Rather than beginning the process of collaborative work search, WE had somehow both become overly focused on me and my ability to earn enough for our new family of four.

Now, I'm not blaming her for this perspective. But it got a little absurd. And the depth of it, with 20-20 reviewing capabilities, goes deeper than I realized while I was married.

Okay, so back to premarital imbalance. I'm a homeowner with some money in the bank. She is not. No worries, we're in this for the long haul.

The thing that really became obvious wasn't obvious until she decided she wanted a divorce.

About six months before the shit hit the fan, the financial shit was still hitting the fan. As we were struggling to make a couple of mortgage payments, I ended up selling $10K of my music equipment to make ends meet. We were stressed out to the max about money. And I thought both of us were working together to find work to support our family.

Maybe she was having a mid-life crisis at that moment. But in this very cash-starved moment in our history together, she was thinking about going into a new field. Okay. And she was casting around for what to do next. Fine.

Thankfully, the Thanksgiving before our divorce, I got an amazing job offer that started up immediately. We were saved. Kind of.

As I began that path of "hi honey, I'm home" fatherhood again, and she was still "searching," something was different. The money was not enough. She was still extremely angry. And really seemed to be directing that anger at me. When the change happened from stress and anxiety to actual focused anger at me, as the problem, I don't know. But it was palpable.

Maybe she was mad that she was still having to look for a job at all. I don't know. I tried asking, but it was fruitless. She was just angry. And when she got angry, she also closed off 100% of the intimacy. I guess that's natural. You can't really make love to someone if you're angry with them. But months would go by, and I'd be the only one seemly noticing that we were not having sex. Like EVER.

So, she was mad. Woke up mad. Went to bed mad. Just mad.

Eventually, this got me a bit angry back and I started looking at the dynamics of our relationship. Here I was working the "good job" again, providing the money and insurance for her to continue her search for "meaningful work," and things were not getting any less stressful between us. What the fuck?

As we moved through the holidays and through January, my job continued to be stressful, and her work search continued to be fruitless. And while the idea of coming home to a happy family and a meal on the stove was kinda cliché, I was hoping for some of the fruits of my labor to be affection.

In February I began voicing my dissatisfaction with the status quo. And while I was primarily talking about our physical closeness and her obvious anger and angry outbursts at me, I was also talking about something more fundamental. In all her angry venting at me, I was beginning to get angry back. I started asking about her job prospects. I started asking about sex. I started asking about dinner when I got home.

And we were having to get our taxes together around this time. And I pushed the final hunting and gathering of the documents on her. I, after all, was working a job that was beginning to kick my ass more than I liked. But I was gung-ho, and we were doing soooo much better, financially.

Then a mini-crisis happened, just in this fragile time, as I'm beginning to stand up for what I needed. I got fired. A wrongful termination suit was brought against my former friend, because I was fired for someone else's mistake, clear as day. But it broke the final ounce of trust and hope from my ex. SHE WAS DONE.

I was not done, I was certain this break would provide a pivot point for us to get back on even footing. For us to finally broach in therapy what was happening in our sexual relationship. But I was the only willing party, at that point. She was finished.

Then two amazing things happened in rapid succession.

1. She found a job (like magic).

2. She showed me the tax return documents for the previous year, and she actually had a negative contribution to the family budget for the year.

BOOM.

The YEAR that we were struggling, the YEAR that I sold two guitars I'd owned for 15+ years to make our mortgage payment, the YEAR that she was mad at my about 90% of the time, was the YEAR that she lost money?

How amazing that the minute she decided she wanted a divorce, her motivation for finding work changed dramatically. Or maybe it was just the marketplace. You tell me.

Anyway, in the divorce, while I chose not to fight about any of the money, I think she came out pretty well. She's got the house. She's got the child support income. (When I get caught back up.) And she's got the kids a large percentage of the time.

I wonder if she's still mad at me. Or if, now, she's found something else to be angry about.

# *Marriage and Money: A Fairy Tale*

Maybe I seemed rich to the first two women who became my wives. Perhaps my downtown condo and simple lifestyle appeared to be something other than it was. I had/have potential, yes, but the real world has a way of changing the game on you, frequently and with indiscriminate outcomes. Maybe the fairy tale went something like this:

1.  Marry a fine gentleman of money.
2.  Have children in a nice house in a top school district.
3.  Stay home and work on parenting and yoga.
4.  Hire weekly housekeeper and part-time nanny.
5.  Live happily ever after.

Something always changes. And when the plans were reset in both marriages, the "stay and home and live the life" part didn't work out as planned. I had hopes. I had means, during various periods in my life. I still have promise and opportunity. To hone in on the mother of my children, there was never any resistance to working. In fact, for much of the early stages of our relationship she made more money than me. (Yay!) And we had a coordinated idea of how we would finance the children and give her the "stay at home" life, as much as possible. We both agreed that we would like one of us (Mom) to meet the bus when the kids began going to school. And when they were infants, well, of course she would stay at home with them. That's how we imagined it.

For the most part, the birthing and getting to school-aged progeny worked. There were some tumbles, mainly 9-11, but we soldiered through as a family. We reached the "meet them at the bus" stage without too much damage to our credit scores. But the dream (examples set by so many lucky wives in our upscale neighborhood) was not fully realized.

She did have to return to part-time work. We still maintained the nanny and housekeeper, but mid-day yoga classes would have to wait. (Bummer.) And I was bummed. I thought that the dream I saw paraded in the grocery store and at our kid's schools, the cars, the house, the fit-happy-zen wife, was supposed to be within my earnings. I needed to earn a bit more.

So I travelled the big corporate route, to seek relief for my suffering and the suffering of my family. But even that wasn't fulfilling the dream. Sure, 20 hours a week beats 50+ with a two-hour daily commute, but it wasn't a competition, it was a cooperation. Still, the dream was suffering. I was suffering. I think the wife was suffering. My suffering had to do with my childhood and my father's extraordinary success. And through many gross legal stories, 15 years after his death, my inheritance was null and void. But I grew up in the most famous house in our town. While things were never very happy there, the outside world must've thought we were living the high life.

Aspire as I might, I won't likely achieve the financial riches my father accomplished by the time he was 40. The fact that he died of a fourth heart attack and cancer at the age of 55 is also not lost on me. But my dad had problems. Mistakes I learned from. Fears I've recoiled from. And a devastating divorce I have striven not to repeat.

Back to me and the ex. So, things change. The big corporate job (which had me getting fatter and more stressed out by the week) went through a major contraction in anticipation of the 2009-2010 financial collapse.

While I saw this as a golden moment to redefine our lifestyles and priorities, my then-wife was panicked. And the road ahead WAS hard. But I imagined that together we would survive and ultimately thrive again. Of course, the economy was hard for everyone, not just us. And the job market was fragmented and getting more ageist by the year. What had been an asset (we're hiring you for some of your wisdom) became a badge of failure.

I was heading towards 50 and interviewing with 30-year-olds. My gray hair had to go. And on the financial front, things didn't work out as planned either. The ex was fired just days after the big corporate layoff was announced. The good news: my fat corporate job provided for six months at full pay, with benefits, and 70% of my annual bonus. The bad news: with the ex out of work, that windfall would be eaten away in three months.

Okay, so the work was set out for us. And it was hard. COBRA payments for child insurance are very high. Occasionally we were paying almost as much for our mortgage. And the job hunt was challenging. At one point, nearing a crisis, I sold most of my music equipment to make a couple of mortgage payments. (It was a bit like O. Henry's story, but I wouldn't know that until later.) Dark times.

And then another fat corporate job came through for me. This time with even more promise and excitement than before. The ex went through some kind of mid-life work reassessment and fished around for multiple job ideas, considered going back to school to learn coding. I shipped off to San Francisco on my first day on the job, to meet the creative team I would be joining. The relief didn't really come soon enough.

The ex was fighting with me on the phone, during my second day in San Francisco. She was demanding to know when the insurance would kick in, when I would get my first full check, and why I had put the room on my credit card. Sure, she was feeling the heat. And sure, she had been paying the bills over the previous six months, while looking to find herself and satisfying work. (That's what we all want, isn't it, "satisfying work?")

But the proof came out later, something I was unaware of, being focused on breadwinning and not the daily bread. When we pulled the information together for the last year of our joint tax return, she actually had a negative contribution to the family budget. WHAT? While I was hammering away and being hammered from both the job and the wife, she was actually losing money?

Tough times, yes, but perhaps her encouragement of my career had just a twinge of self-motivation behind it. See, if I would just get that big corporate job again, we could return to normal, "meet the bus after school" part-time livin'. Except that's not what happened.

**Note:** After an early morning chat with my talky therapist, I've come up with a catchphrase to frame the renewed attitude of detachment from my ex and her future struggles. "Oh, I'm sorry that didn't work out for you." It's more compassion than I ever got from her while I was struggling and certainly more than I got yesterday. I guess I have to consider the worst outcome and at least have that in mind. I suppose she could have me thrown in jail for not giving her the money I don't have. I'm already skating above bankruptcy and just trying to keep a roof over my head and the heads of my children. But I suppose she might do it.

# The Close of Business Between Us: Taking Back the Heart of Darkness

It wasn't too long ago, six months I guess, that I was feeling a moment of pause, reflection, and doubt. During a kid drop-off moment, I had the idea, "If I'm going to start completely over with someone, I'd rather start completely over with my ex." Not to remarry, or move back into my old house (we'd certainly gone too far for that), but to actively date for a bit. She was still the one person I wanted to chat with more than anyone. And it wasn't about sex, although at that moment I had not been with anyone else.

I wrote her an open email about where I was standing. Professed my continued love for her and proposed we discuss, imagine, see if something like "dating" would appeal to her as well. I was pretty sure at that point that her "other lovers" totalled about two, but only one had been confirmed.

But it wasn't from a place of weakness or sorrow. Actually it was a place of great strength. I was thinking, "I'm big enough to tell her this." And a funny thing happened when I sent the email. I was actually able to let go of any expectations of what the result would be. In fact, in many ways, I was releasing her with one final ask, "Are you sure this is what you want? Because it is STILL NOT WHAT I WANT."

The silence was deafening. About 36 hours later she responded with, "I'm very touched by your offer." And some more blah blah blah. It was a resounding NO.

But even before she responded, I was feeling a huge lift. In a way that I had not felt since she asked for the divorce, I was feeling free of her. I clarified after her ho-hum response. I was not looking to move back in or really change the current living or even kid schedule, I was merely imagining that we might want to spend some time getting to know each other again, before we truly moved on.

It was clear from her lack of follow-up that I was the one still wanting to get to know her. Her last missive on the subject alluded to how I was a "very desirable man" and ... blah blah blah... She was not interested.

A few weeks later we made plans to do the kid's Christmas presents together in my house. She would come to my house, since I had the first half of the holiday in our schedule. I could not have done this had I not had this release.

At the end of the second message I mentioned going out on the open dating market for the first time. (I don't know why I needed to put that in.) And sure enough, within a few weeks I was aligned with my dog-loving ice breaker.

Today, many months later, she has let me know she has been seeing her new lover since December. At least that gives me the idea that she was really in a place to consider my reconnect offer. Who knows.

And as she discovered my blog (thanks to Google's advertising efforts), I now have even less to talk about. I don't disdain her. Far from it. But there is a completion to my process with her. I don't really want to see her when I drop off the kids. I don't like her renewed fantastic shoe fetish, or her recut short blonde hairdo. I'd rather not... Not even imagine.

And a helpful concept from the divorce recovery class comes to mind often in our "drop-off" encounters.

"Think of your ex as a convenience store clerk. You are there to conduct business and leave. You don't need to exchange pleasantries or ask how things are going."

In fact, I'm best not knowing any of the details of her life.

So six months ago, I negotiated our final close of business. And now we are free to date, love, enjoy. And, as she has been in this entire process, she's still just a few steps ahead of me.

# THROWN TO THE WOLVES

And then things were forever changed. She filed her case with the Attorney General's office. And we were suddenly in a legal battle again, and I went from struggling and working and not making enough money to a "deadbeat dad."  But that wasn't enough. I was also now nearing default on my mortgage. I again pleaded with her to give me some options. She began her new response, "I signed an agreement with the AG's office not to negotiate about money with you." END OF DISCUSSION.

As the last year began to close, it became clear that she was blocking my attempts to file restructuring bankruptcy to try and keep the Gnome House. I looked to my mom for some financial support, but she really hadn't like the house from the beginning. Fuck. I was out of options and receiving newly threatening weekly letters from the AG's office. It was time to sell. And without a full-time big corporate job, I didn't have the income to even look for a place to move to. At 51 years old I was heading back under the roof of my mom. The shame was palpable, but what were my options?

# On the Turning Away: Fighting with Your Ex About Money

We give and we give and we try to find ways to mend, and sometimes it is not enough. While we are married we try to adapt. But after the vows are broken, it can get ugly.

Today I am angry and I'm going to rant for a second.

I have some money in the bank, and I owe my ex-wife some back child support. BUT… I can't pay her. I mean, technically I could, even though she's asked me to deal with the Attorney General's office going forward, so there's that. And I need to start paying her again, and I will.

Today I am saving my cash to pay the retainer on a lawyer rather than paying money to my ex for my kids. This sucks. I have tried everything but begging to get my ex to stop battering me with threats, but of course, now it's too late, the paperwork has been filed, and shortly I'll be on the AG's list for back child support issues.

It was never an issue of willingness. I have not been holding out or hiding money from my ex. It's the same crash landing advice we've been hearing on airplanes for years. The part about the seat cushion being a floatation device and the more relevant part, "Put your mask on first and then help your child."

You see, there's this little matter of food and shelter that outweighs even the wrath of my ex-wife. I wasn't trying to hide or be an asshole about it, I was being quite upfront about the problem as soon as I knew there might be a shortfall. But she no longer has to listen to me or take my side of the story as a partner. Now I'm just the deadbeat dad who's not paying his child support.

But wait. Again, this is a simplification of a very complex issue. When my business took a turn in May, I began renewed efforts to find work, and even full-time employment, abandoning the business I've been building back up for the last three years.  And though we didn't use attorneys to fight over the kids or the divorce, she's now perfectly willing to call foul and throw me to the system for deadbeat dads.

The good news is, a family attorney assured me that the court would hear and understand my side of the story. The goal of the court would be to make sure we had a plan in place to make her financially whole again before my daughter's 18th birthday, when the child support obligations would need to be satisfied in full. WAIT. What did he say?

So while I'm about to put money into the pockets of the legal system rather than my ex-wife and children's, there is some good news. In my case, it's clear I have been trying to work out a deal with her. I even offered a full agreement of her accounting, including incidentals and miscellaneous if she would come to the table without having to hire attorneys. There was no reason not to, it's how we settled our divorce.

But for some reason, she chose the quick out. "The AG's office made me sign a letter that I would not negotiate with you on child support."

So tonight, with money in the bank, I am still short on amassing the small fortune required for my attorney's retainer. Fuck. That's so wrong. That's NOT where this money should go. EVER.

So tonight, a full flip of the bird to the ex who still refuses to negotiate in good faith and would rather pitch it to the state than talk to me. At least I like the guy who's going to represent me. And did you know we're likely not to see the courtroom for three to six months? More BS.

So to you, dear ex, there is no reason for this. You even admit that I'm not trying to hide money from you. But you'd rather pay attorney's fees, and yes, you will probably require some representation of your own, than simply getting along with our lives as best as we can.

Request to other moms in similar situations: Make a note of who your former husband is and if he was honest and forthcoming while you were married to him, and when there are hardships, sit down and talk things over. Because throwing things to the state, or the lawyers, especially if you have a willing ex-partner who is open to sharing and problem solving, is stupid. And it makes parenting issues more difficult. How can I be flexible and loving when you ask for adjustments to the parenting plan, when you're suing me in court?

I know there are couples who find themselves in situations where attorneys are the only way to go. But I've never tried to hide my situation or shirk my liabilities and responsibilities. So why now? What's got the bee in your bonnet now? Didn't you get the Standard Possession Order just like you wanted? The house, just like you wanted? Even the amount of the child support, just like you wanted?

Well, squeezing me out of my house and home is not a viable solution, and now I'm going to fight back. The money that I should be paying to you, right now, tonight, I'm saving for a legal retainer. AGAIN, not to fight the amount or the obligation but simply to slow down the court system you activated from making my financial recovery (and thus YOUR FINANCIAL RECOVERY) more difficult.

You CAN sue your ex and ask for a weekend swap in the same breath, but it sure sucks, for all of us.

# Terms of Surrender: Our Divorce Papers

Under the terms of my surrender, I gave up a good portion of my time with my kids. I was under the impression that this was the path that was "best for the kids." In fact, it was the path that was best for my ex-wife, the person in the marriage who decided she wanted out. So wait, under the terms of my surrender I am giving her the kids, the house, and a good stipend of my income for the next 11 years? Just a minute, I need to reconsider.

Of course, reconsideration was not an option. When one person decides he or she is done, the marriage is done. Sure, you could counsel or work things out, for a bit, but once the door has been smashed open, the exit is always a possibility. And now a threat. And in the case of divorce, just a matter of fact, please sign on the dotted line and be done with this business.

Wait.

We chose an uncontested divorce. I agreed to her request for a divorce, because fighting would be expensive, might damage our children, and would echo the hurt still in my young-boy mind from my parents' brutal divorce struggle. So I went with the path of least resistance, I bowed my neck at the correct time, and allowed the head of my shining promise to be sliced off with little drama or prior bloodshed. That's the way it was supposed to be, right? That's what we were after.

But something along the way was not quite explained to me until a few months ago. I was on a date with a woman who had just given up primary custody, and she was saying how much better her ex had become once he had to actually do 50% of the parenting rather than complaining about a check and doing nothing. I remember distinctly my reaction, "Wait, what? He doesn't pay you any child support?"

So if I get this straight, my high-priced divorce counselor, who advised me to just take the deal and get on with the divorce, forgot to mention that the non-custodial parent pays child support. Why didn't my counselor listen or fight for my request to go for 50/50? Why didn't she support the discussion about 50/50 parenting? She didn't. Why didn't she?

I guess I ultimately need to ask her. But in reconnecting with my attorney (the one who I contacted re my wife's newfound righteousness in turning me over to the Attorney General's office), he said this: "In 2010 when you guys divorced, she was probably right. Your wife would've probably gotten exactly what she wanted. Not that you couldn't have gone for 50/50. But today, things are a little different. Even in Texas. The judges today are listening when the parents want 50/50 custody. And more often than not, my dad clients are getting it, if they fight for it."

Well, that is good news for today's dads. Not so good for yesterday's dads, or me.

What are my options today? Reopen the fight, go prove I'm a worthy dad, and ask the judges and the court to readjust my custody to 50/50? Is that what I want?

Here are the potential consequences:

- It will cost us both a lot of money. Money that we tried not to spend in divorce, by consulting a wonderful PhD divorce counselor.

- It might damage my wife's ability to continue to afford the house we bought together.

- My kids might get the impression I am fighting their mom

or saying she's doing something wrong.

- It will cause drama and hardship on all sides.

Here are the benefits:

- The $150,000+ would still be going to my kids.
- I would be able to afford housing and perhaps not be forced to work two jobs or give my life back up to the big corporate job.
- We could parent 50/50 just like we are doing now, but I also would be able to help with some of the clothes and supplies shopping.
- My kids would know that I wanted them 50/50 from the beginning and was asked to take less.

As of this writing I don't have the money to pursue the court's resolution of my 50/50 desires. I wish our counselor had supported both of our requests with the same integrity. I wish my 50/50 parenting plans and 50/50 schedules had been taken seriously while we were negotiating our peace treaty. They were not. I was given the patronizing approval, "that's nice" but "that's not how it's going to work out." And then I was told to accept what's "in the best interest of the children."

Bullshit.

I was sold a bill of goods by my then-wife, who had been consulting with her attorney, and our counselor, who was found and selected by my wife. And then I was asked to sign the Terms of Surrender without being given the full story of custody and child support. My bad. I should have paid for my own attorney at that point, rather than stumble along blindly with the hope of good will, good intentions, and honesty.

I got none of the above. What I got was a temporary peace treaty that lasted until I was late on my second child support payment to my ex-wife. Then the courts of the great state of Texas were warmed up against me. And today, according to my attorney, I could be arrested at any time, by the Attorney General's office. That is certainly part of the Terms of Surrender that I signed, but it's not in line with the honest and caring approach we took to setting up our peaceful retreat from the marriage.

I'm defeated a bit at the moment. But I'll get back up, I always do.

## *Attorney General's Office Round 2: Deadbeat Dad – 0, Bank – $43,000*

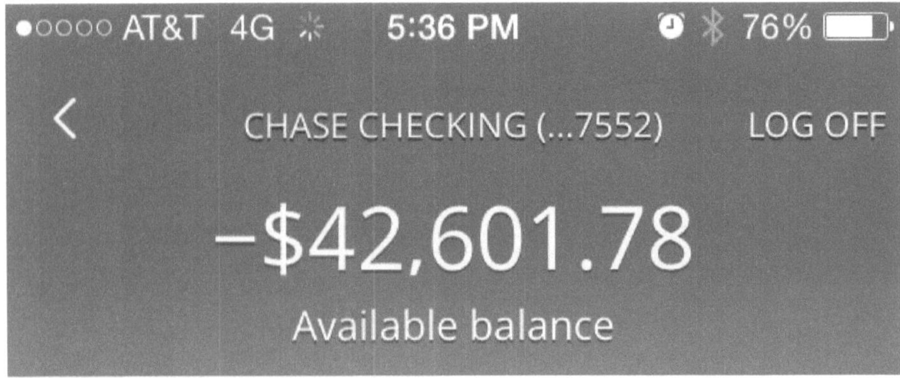


This evening, after picking my kids up and having dinner at a local restaurant, the waitress handed back my credit card back: "It's been declined." Um, what? I had just been talking to a client about their credit card number being stolen and used in Mexico in a fraud transaction, and that's what crossed my mind when I opened the banking app to see this lovely number presented to me. I even showed it to the kids, claiming I had accidentally bought a used BMW and just forgot to transfer the funds to cover it.

I was joking. The good news is my daughter had some cash to buy school clothes with this weekend, so we had some money. I was essentially frozen out. Nada.

Back at the house, my sister's house where we are staying this weekend, I was informed a legal hold had been placed on my account. After a few humiliating conversations I was given the Attorney General's office number, where I could plead my case.

The timing is concurrent with my ex filing her case against me. I texted her since we've been talking again lately, strategizing about insurance and such, until I get my next big gig. I let her know I didn't think she did it, but I needed to ask. She was very happy that I gave her the benefit of the doubt, but she had not done anything else. No, the damage was done a year ago. The hurt that had rained down on me since.

I told her, "You walk away from the marriage, but you can't walk away from the financial enmeshment. Like it or not, we're still dependant on the other's earning power. I've been doing everything I can to find the next opportunity for my work. And I would tell you that I'm not worried. But again, I might have delusions of grandeur. I've been working on replacing this income since June."

So in the best interest of the children, she filed suit against me with the Attorney General's office. And over the course of the next few months, I began to struggle to keep the house over my head, while continuing to look for more work, or enough work to pay her child support.

I guess the real story is this: I am still struggling to take my income up high enough that I can afford to have a place to live and pay her child support. And while we are essentially parenting at 50/50 levels, I am still the non-custodial parent. And when you call that number the AG's office gives you, you identify as the custodial or non-custodial parent. There's no gray area in the eyes of the law.

I'm guessing there's a little gray area in the eyes of my readers unless you've been through something like this. I state as fact that I am not hiding money, I am not trying to skip out of my responsibility, and I am not shirking my parenting duties in any way. I am 100% available to my kids and to my ex for support and care. I still have not managed to get the corporate job that will afford us both a better life. But that's the deal, right? Even after the divorce, we are still in this financial relationship forever. Our kids are going to need cars, and rent, and tuition, and food money, and … the ex and I will negotiate those things as well.

But today the force of the law has come to visit me, rendering me penniless in addition to homeless. (Not to be too dramatic, we're not under a bridge, but we're living with my family.) As the ex was contemplating her move to file against me, she was making a decision to put everything I had accomplished up to that point at risk. And in the bet, I lost. I lost it all. I am starting over again, from zero. Oh, and the amount is not indicative of how much I owe, it's two or three times over the amount ordered.

Still, we will struggle on. And still, I will attempt to keep the fighting to a minimum. And still, I will struggle to find my next big job so I can afford to help her afford the nice house in the nice neighborhood we bought with my downpayment and salary for 11 years. No problem, it's really the kid's house, in my mind. Except she's got all the keys.

And now she's got me in some kind of death grip lien until I'm able to get in touch with my lawyer and respond. Again, this is money we should not be fighting over. This is money that should not go to a lawyer, but to our kids. I made several attempts to secure the back payment with a lien against a piece of property I own that is for sale. I am not attempting to skip a debt. But the state is now attempting to collect the debt I owe her.

What an interesting start to the new school year. I laughed and told the kids it was some weird bank thing. They don't need to be involved or informed about what's really taking place. Nor will they know, until they are older, that their mom's actions cost me the house as well.

Onward and upward. It's the first night since school started that I've seen them, so we're doing homework.

Here's how our text went regarding this new development.

Today, 6:10 PM

Just curious, have you taken any new action with the AG's office? Or perhaps they are just acting on their own? They've now frozen my bank account completely. Talking to my atty tomorrow, oh well. I'm guessing it's just them...

Today, 6:14 PM

oh ⬤, that blows. Thanks for giving me the benefit of the doubt. Indeed I have not done anything new re the AG. Maybe they have automatic calendars re process?

yeah, no worries. I figured since we're talking, you wouldn't have done anything else... thanks for the info

oh of course

I guess if she'd said she was sorry, she'd be admitting that it was a mistake. Obviously, she doesn't think it's a mistake or feels the need to apologize. What am I expecting?

# The Fuck You that Keeps on Giving

Today I am angry. It takes a lot to get me urgent and angry. My sense of urgency has been triggered at this point. I am sitting in my mom's house with a $43,000 hold on my credit card (about triple the disputed child support amount). I can't get my lawyer on the phone. I wonder what would happen if I were thrown in jail by the Attorney General's office rather than just frozen out of any access to my money. I guess I need to plan for the worst and understand what my options are.

I am grateful that I'm not in jail at this moment.

But I have to say, this sure has done a lot to dampen my optimistic outlook today. I'll be back above it shortly, but at the moment, I am essentially paralyzed. It's better here on my mom's couch, with AC, electricity, and a strong wifi signal. But I'm a bit tranquil for the situation.

I'm not exactly sure how I came to have this low level of reactivity. I guess my father's response would've been to blow up at everyone possible. And maybe my lack of blowup-ness is part of my anti-dad training. I'm feeling a bit defeated. A bit dead.

And what I know about myself is that these feelings are the harbingers of depression. Fuck that! The opposite of depression is high energy and activation. So today, I'm going to fire up the jets and get mad. What's the risk? There's nothing more that she could do to me, other than have me thrown in jail, and I guess it's really not up to her, right?

Except the coup de grâce was hers. In some sense of fear or entitlement (the opposite sides of a coin as well), she decided it was better to attack me than negotiate and talk to me. Somewhere in her muddled little mind, she took the path of war. And in all the work I've done to get healthy, this is the one attack that I still have a hard time accepting. Divorce me, sure. Expect and count on the child support, yes. But when one of us stumbles, as a divorced couple, as co-parents, the response HAS GOT TO BE HELP, NOT ATTACK.

I stumbled. I am still stumbling forward. And rather than deal with me, or hear my plea for patience, my ex took the harshest action at her disposal and filed against me with the AG's office. The machine was started and the damage is still being inflicted.

Today I will respond in kind. For the first time since my marriage began to crumble, I am genuinely mad at my ex-wife.

There is no reason to attack a parent who is being transparent and cooperative.

When there are financial hardships on either side of the divorce, the impact is felt by everyone.

If your reaction to your ex-partner's struggle is to attack them, you have lost touch with any and all compassion you once had for them.

Attacking your ex-partner for any reason hurts your kids.

Is it always the best approach to be the bigger partner and not fight back? Is it always the best approach to maintain a positive outlook and find the pro-active solution? Or at some point, do you need to pull out your own guns and fire back? I'm not sure I know the answer to this. For over four years I have been taking the buddhist approach and attempting to rise above the blame and anger and NOT attack my ex-wife FOR ANY REASON.

Today, I don't know. The lawyer, when he finally calls me back, will have to advise me.

First blood, second blood has been drawn. At this point, I'm a bit like the Evil Black Knight in Monty Python's Holy Grail.  He is still taunting his enemy when he has lost both arms and legs. I am standing on my stumps at the moment, and I've got nothing else to defend myself with. And today I will shout my anger to the hills. Perhaps at some point I will (to use a very different metaphor) FLAME ON, like the human torch.

At my son's cross-country meeting at the middle school this morning, she stopped me in the hall. I was certain she was going to say she was sorry. She wanted to tell me something about the kid's acne medicine. Um, yeah, thanks, and fuck you.

This is not my natural or comfortable state. It's like I have to spin up the anger momentum for a while before I actually get angry. I am certain that I learned this subversion of anger from the overbearing and abusive anger of my father. He shouted the anger right out of all of us. I see my sister and mother get terrified when I get angry with them. I have to stop for a minute and reassure them, "It's okay, this is what healthy anger looks like." They look at me with deer-in-the-headlights expressions.

But it really is okay to be angry. And as a counter-measure to depression, anger is a powerful tool.

And I guess, since this episode started at 6:00 p.m., and I still haven't heard back from my lawyer, I'll have a touch of anger to give him as well.

There's plenty of anger to go around, I've got enough for everyone. Still, I am cautious not to lash out. Today is one of countermeasures and planning, not vengeance. That is better taken when the dust has settled and the evening sun is setting over the battlefield.

# I'm No Divorce Expert, but if You Parent 50/50, You Should Divorce 50/50

I'm kinda sick of the divorce experts and family law (meaning un-family law) solicitors who hover around the business of divorce. The only problem is, it is a business. And divorce is a business decision. And without some good counsel, you might get screwed. Still, calling yourself a divorce expert sounds really stupid to me. I want to ask them, "Oh, so how many divorces have you been through, and which one turned you magically into an expert?"

I'm no expert, I'm no advice columnist, I'm no self-help blogger. If you're heading towards or in the middle of a divorce, I recommend you get some help on your side. And provided you are not in a high-conflict divorce situation, you might include your future-ex in the discussions about finding counsel. That's not exactly how the sequence went down in either of my divorces, but that ultimately became the intention and result. We wanted to collaborate on our divorce, not drag each other through the legal halls shedding thousands of dollars along the way.

Here's the big *ah-ha* for me about divorce: If one partner wants a divorce, there's not much hope for a reconciliation. In the case of my second marriage, when the partner has consulted a divorce attorney before raising the issue with you, you're pretty well on your way to being handed a divorce whether you want it or not. I didn't. It didn't matter. We're divorced. I'm getting over it.

The second *ah-ha* about divorce was this: How you got into the divorce process is probably how it's going to go. In my case, my then-wife consulted an attorney, even while we were actively in couple's therapy, suggesting a major emotional disconnect that was not going to be resolved in the divorce. But knowing this was where she was coming from, that even with a counselor involved she was not able to get her needs met, I was able to let her go more easily. I knew that nothing I had done had caused her to seek a divorce. In fact, I was doing everything I could to keep the marriage together. I was working harder. I was improving my chore-tackling attitude. I was trying to be more empathetic to her complaints. But the complaints were getting longer, and it seemed like our therapy sessions stayed focused on these surface "you didn't do" issues rather than the kind of tectonic hurts that drove her to seek divorce advice before letting me know she was leaning away from our marriage. I was shocked and hurt when she admitted the fact in therapy, but I immediately had a better understanding of this person who was asking for her exit pass.

If you've got kids you've got to make them the focus of the hopefully-peaceful divorce. In our case, the kids did come first, though I might have negotiated things differently had I been less empathetic. Heading into the new kind of therapy session, the one where we were writing the rules of our divorce, I was disoriented and depressed. We even stopped the negotiations for a week as I made my case to my wife about why I didn't want the divorce. We then moved along towards a parenting plan with her help. At least I got the moment of pause and reflection. But I could see in my wife's face and hear in her responses that she was done. Done done. Not just done.

So we quickly moved to the logistics of the divorce. I came with a plan to go for 50/50 custody. My wife had other plans. And unfortunately, in my state, Texas, the laws were very much on the mother's side in 80% of all divorces. I understand from my new lawyer that in 2019 things are looking up for the dad who wants 50/50 custody. It appears the judges are more likely to hear both sides of the story and make a ruling that is based on desire and fairness rather than legal precedent.

Unfortunately, I got divorced in 2010. The legal precedent was with the mom all the way. And our divorce counselor quickly moved our discussions to how things would look with me being the non-custodial dad, and how the "time was not really all that different." What I did not know, and I did not have an attorney tell me, so listen up, was this:  If I had gotten 50/50 parenting, as I wanted, I would not be forced to pay child support. We would do our own thing, we would pay our own way, and we would part as 50/50 responsible co-parents, just as we had parented. But that's not what happened.

I did my research. I brought books and selected copies from those books to our sessions. I drew up some creative 50/50 schedules. And I was politely humored, but somewhere, in the cabal of women, they both knew I would give in to reason. Or the powerful sounding, "in the best interest of the children."

Wait a minute.

I understood that the kids needed both a mom and a dad. And I also understood that at the moment my soon-to-be-ex was making more money than I was. And I was paying this counselor to represent my side of the case as well.

And somewhere along the way, perhaps when things looked a bit more locked up than she was used to, our "impartial counselor" suggested to me, "That's what she'll get if you go to court."

Yes, but...

Today I can look back and see I was railroaded. Perhaps in the name of efficiency and lowering the conflict, I was given the verdict. Settle for the non-custodial role, or go to court and pay to be given the non-custodial role. This sucked. But again, I was depressed, I was living in my sister's house, away from the kids, and I was desperate to get on with whatever life we would have after the business of the divorce was settled. So, I succumbed. I agreed to the Standard Possession Order and the non-custodial role that was offered to me. And the negotiations went pretty quickly from there. To be honest, I just wanted out of the meetings with my still-wife. I was still in love with her. I was holding back all efforts to plead with her. And her steely eyes showed me she had other plans. She was more prepared for the divorce negotiations because she had been thinking about it, and maybe even planning her actions, long before I was aware there was a divorceable-rift in our marriage.

"This often happens to the dads," our counselor told us. "They are not aware there is a broken marriage until the divorce is in progress. And they are often slower to accept the breakup."

Um… Yeah. I was fighting from within the strength of my marriage one minute and then being told she'd already consulted an attorney. Those are two different universes in my life. I was struggling to let go of the first one and begin to accept the second one. The universe where she would go on to be with other men, where I wouldn't see my kids every night, where I was going to be alone again.

Divorce is the most painful and life-transforming thing that I've ever been through. Perhaps as each of your kids comes into the world, your life is transformed, and you grow into a parent. But as a divorcing parent, you are looking at losing a good portion of your kids' lives. No way around it. The pictures my ex-wife takes of the kids are always painful. The vacations they now take without me, with their mom's boyfriend, are always a bit tender. I don't really want to see them. I'm glad they had fun. I'm very happy when they return. But it's like two different lives they lead.

So we decide to divorce, or one person decides, and then we divorce. Our kids' worlds are split into two parallel universes: one that they experience with dad and one that they experience with mom. Suddenly they have two homes. Maybe a new person in their parent's life that they have to adjust to. The stories they tell around the dinner table are no longer shared in both universes. There's Mom's universe and Dad's universe.

As parents, divorced parents, we have to do our best to fill in the gaps alone. As our kids are away, doing other great things, we have to keep our chins up and our spirits positive as we look towards building our own lives, now separate from them and their mom. It's okay, I'm not whining. We all make it. But there were a few things I didn't know going into the early part of the divorce process. And this most significant thing that our "divorce expert" failed to tell me was also the part that has caused me the most pain and drama. 50/50 shared parents don't pay child support to each other.

The Two Laws of Divorce:

1.  Kids first.
2.  If you parent 50/50, you should divorce 50/50.

Without exception, especially if one of you wants it, you should push for 50/50 parenting. If the other person is unwilling to give up 50% of their parenting time, perhaps they need to reconsider the decision to divorce. That would not have made a difference in my then-wife's decision to divorce me, but it would have had a significant impact on my ability to thrive financially post-divorce. I was asking for the half parenting for purely emotional reasons. I cannot say what my then-wife had in mind, but she'd gotten some legal advice by this time, and I had not.

Do not go into divorce naively. Get informed. I came to my divorce counseling meetings with books, information, scholarly articles, and I still lost the negotiations. Today I would not make the same mistake. I am telling you this story so you don't make this same mistake.

If you want 50/50 parenting and are ready in your heart and mind to step up to the large task of co-parenting, then you should go for it. For the health and well-being of your kids, I hope you get it.

# Losing Everything in Divorce and Learning to Carry on

Can a man survive without a home? Without a job? Without his family? Divorce often feels like the end of your life. And, of course, it is the end of life as you have known it up to that time. Post-divorce life is very different for everyone. And, as water continues to flow under the bridge, some of the life-threatening blows become less severe.

The first death-blow for me was losing my house. Of course, it was a lot more than a house. The house we created for our family was filled with our hopes and dreams. It was the physical manifestation of our plans as a couple with kids on the way. We bought the house for our future family. And everything we became in the years within the house was our family history BD (before divorce). As a symbolic loss, a house is very important. The money, the commitment, the work that went into buying and maintaining the house... It was the only home I knew for my family. Walking out, or being asked to leave, was the first life-threatening loss in a long series of future losses.

Can a man survive without a home? As a single dad with the Standard Possession Order, it is possible to survive for a while without a home. For me, I was able to find shelter at my sister's house. I was homeless but I had shelter. I was even able to have my kids on my weekends. And we made it work. But it was not easy.

A few of the intangibles you lose when you lose your house go beyond the material goods. Sure there are a lot of "things" that you lose, that you wouldn't even know how to ask for, but there is so much more to the loss. For me, I lost my neighborhood, full of green-belts and parks, and home to the tennis club where I played three times a week. The dream that we had created was working for me. And now it was lost.

Can a man survive without a job?

The second death blow. This one is tougher. With today's economy this struggle for solvency is much more difficult than I remember it ever being in the past. Of course, now I have an additional $1,500 a month in expenses, and that puts even more pressure on my employment. And, if I want to have a place to live, it requires a much higher salary base. As long as I have the BIG JOB, I can have a place to live and pay my child support. But when things get even a bit tight, something will suffer.

As things went for me, I was lucky. After a few months of living with my sister, I got another BIG JOB and felt like I was off to the races of picking my life back up, as a man and father. Of course, I want a home for my kids. And of course, I want my ex-wife to be able to afford the home I left. I want them both. And I am willing to work to support both dreams. So off I went on my new job, and I immedi-ately set out to buy a new home for myself and my kids. It was a rite of passage. I needed to establish another home. I needed a place for my things again.

And things were good for a few months. I got my home, I got my kids in my new home. We swam at the nearby lake, we jumped on the new trampoline, we became a family, a single-dad family, once again.

But things changed, and my employer changed business models and eliminated my position. Six months in, on my new mortgage, I was jobless again. For a while, I was able to make ends meet by cash-ing in my retirement funds and my savings. I landed some contracts and some project work. And I made my payments and my mortgage as best as I could. For the next year and a half, things lurched along with some sacrifices and some drama, but for the most part, I was able to say on top of the money situation.

And things changed again. As my primary contract changed my billable hours, I saw that I would be late paying my ex-wife on the child support. I contacted her to let her know what was going on. And we were okay for the first month. However, things did not get better with my work. And the loss of hours was not immediately replaced.

It was in the second month of my delay that my ex-wife began threatening to turn it all over to the Attorney General's office. I asked her to reconsider. She pressed. We devolved into angry exchanges over email. We were both sure that we were right.

In the end, she did turn all of our financial details over to the AG's office. She had some reason. She was doing the best she could for her family, I suppose, but it was very hard for me to reconcile her actions while continuing to cooperate on all the parenting tasks. We agreed that the money fight should not affect our parenting. And we did okay with that.

But when I lost my steady income, or it dropped to an amount lower than my survival rate, I did not have any backup funds, I had no safety net.

In the end, I was unable to replace the income loss from my main work contract. And I was unsuccessful at supplementing that income enough to get caught back up on my mortgage or my child support. And now with the AG's office putting the credit screws on me, I was unable to refinance or file for restructuring bankruptcy. I lost my house. Well, I got to sell my house, but it was not what I wanted.

So now, I'm homeless again. And I have this same choice to make. I can go for the BIG JOB and make enough money to have my own place and support their mom in keeping our old house. Or I can fight in the courts for 50/50 parenting, what I wanted in the first place, and reduce my primary expenses by $1,500 a month.

Today I am interviewing for the BIG JOB. And I am hopeful to return to full employment in the next few weeks. And I will begin making my child support payments as soon as that is possible. But today, I am without a home. I am without a job.

I am surviving on goodwill, guts, and hopefulness.

# What an Angry or Distant Divorced Parent Looks Like

I'm not that guy. I have never exited my role as a father. While I am no longer in a marriage with my ex-wife, I am very much available to her for support, flexible child care, advice, and parenting. That's what we do. That's what we did all along. Even in our pre-kid relationship, we were reading books about 50/50 parenting and attachment parenting. We entered this relationship together as hopeful parents, and now as divorced parents something else has come into play.

I've seen what an angry and distant father looks like after divorce. My dad, though an alcoholic, exited the marriage with an enormous amount of anger and vitriol hurled back at all of us. He was unaware how his tirades against my mom also felt like attacks against me. He was not very self-aware, but alcoholics are usually not all that introspective. He was an asshole. He fought about money all the time, even though he was making a ton of it.

It was the principle of the thing, he would say, from time to time. Once he confronted me, while I was in high school and staying at his house over Spring Break. "You may not love me," he yelled. "But you're damn well gonna respect me." Sounds like a bad movie, right? The words were seared into my brain forever. I vowed never to put myself in that position with my father again. And until he was dying of cancer, and no longer able to drink, we never spent another night under the same roof.

I know there are vindictive fathers. I know there are high-conflict divorces. Ours was not one of those. Even in divorce we negotiated. The horror of my parent's divorce was not going to be visited on my children, or even on my ex-wife. And as I compromised what I was asking for, 50/50 parenting, I was told that's what I would get any-way, so I'd better just accept it and move on. Um, WHAT?

Turns out that in 2009 when we were divorcing, 80% of all divorces in Texas ended up with the dad getting non-custodial parent and the every-other-weekend Standard Possession Order schedule. (Stan-dard Possession Order, once you've heard of it, you'll never forget it.) So that's what I was handed as my option. And since we had agreed not to fight, I complied. I did not fight my then-wife in the nego-tiations for the custody of our children. I did not argue when the amount of child support was calculated on my previous job at Dell, even though I was looking for my next job. I didn't fight. I sublimated my anger and frustration into some abstract support for my chil-dren. By not fighting and providing all this money for my children, things would be a little better for them then it was for me, when I was a kid. Okay, a LOT better.

But as I've written, things didn't work out the way we planned. The eminent job from 3M, then HP, then Dell again, didn't happen. The economy was tanking, and a 50-ish tech marketing executive was not in high demand. So I struggled to find my footing as a provider, post-divorce. It was okay, I would catch back up. I would replace my retirement savings that I was sucking down at an alarming rate to make the child support payments, even though I didn't have a job.

And we, the nuclear family, continued on. And my employment has had ups and downs, as has the employment of my ex-wife. But somehow, we're still tied together in the original decree that speci-fied an amount of child support that was in alignment with my job between 2007 and 2009, and a long way from where I am today.

But the part that is perplexing, is where my ex began to fear that I was going to skip out on my child support payments. Or that per-haps she needed to take more aggressive action to collect the child support, in the name of "supporting the children." Huh?

Somewhere in her post-divorce mind she had concocted an inner-story that I was trying to screw her out of the money. I was telling her exactly what was happening with me and reassuring her about the money. Eventually, I would get the big job again, and payments would resume and repayment plans would be put in place. I was NEVER disputing the money. I was even willing to continue to go into debt to her at the Dell-salary clip, when we both knew that this was not in line with what I was making. I was trying to do what was right by my kids, first and foremost. The money was not important, in the long run. The absence of conflict was more important.

And tonight I had some hilarious conversations with my kids about the -$42,000 problem with my credit card. My son is determined to figure out what happened. I've told them it's not something I can discuss with them. And we joked about my drug habit, or the cool condo I had rented downtown for when they weren't with me. They knew I was joking. But they were also concerned or curious what had zapped my credit card with such a huge debt.

Eventually my kids will know what happened. That the actions of their mom, against me, for no good reason, caused me to lose my house and have all of my financial assets frozen. The last step I guess is jail. At that point, I suppose my mom or someone would have to pay my child support (it's nothing near $43,000 by the way; the state usually goes for triple damages as a start).

It's funny, she is really asking me to be a 50/50 parent all the time, by complaining about how many appointments she has to schedule and how she's always the one responsible to remember school requirements and such. But those are exactly the kind of things she'd be mad at me about if we were still married. I'm glad we are not. She's still mad about them.

At the moment, I am on a cash-only basis. I have no bank account. My attorney said, "They're going to keep that account. You might as well forget that money and open another account somewhere else."

For my ex-wife, somehow it became about the money rather than the kids. It's certainly not about 50/50 parenting, since the Standard

Possession Order is more like 70/30. (If you account for the impossibility of taking the kids for an entire month in the summer.)

When did my ex-wife get so adversarial that rather than support me in a difficult time, she'd rather hammer me into pulp and hope for the best? Get part of something or all of nothing. Today there is nothing.

When you get divorced, there is no separation of the financial obligations you still have to support your family. If there is a huge imbalance in incomes, perhaps the wealthier party should have to pay some supportive money to the stay-at-home mom, or in our case the working mom who wants to continue to live in the upscale house in the upscale neighborhood and school district in the "best interest of the children." Yes. But if you crush the father with unreasonable debt and legal action, what do you get then?

Nothing.

There's a funny moment, that illustrates the "off" thinking. We were meeting with an accountant who specializes in helping couples divide their money for a divorce. My then-wife was furious that I had bought a new (very used) car. She kept coming back to it with the accountant. "But how can he rack up this new debt and we still have to split it?"

The accountant carefully pointed out, "Your car is worth about $3,000 more than the car he just purchased. And your car will be paid off in eight months. It all works out in the math." Still, she was angry, as if I had purchased a car just to shift some of my debt onto her.

So she's still mad. She will probably be mad for the rest of our kids' lives. At least she's not telling them all the time that she's mad at me. And that's the pact, for now. God bless us, everyone.

# ALL THINGS
# COLLAPSE

In March 2014, I sold my home and moved in to my mom's house. OUCH. My mom and I laughed through the situation with a phrase, "Well, it beats living under a bridge." Yes, it does. But it didn't have to go this way.

Somewhere in the divorce she had lost all compassion for me. When my house was being threatened by foreclosure she pressed the entire issue, her issue, to the AG's office, thus obstructing any potential remedy I might seek. And in the loss, my kids and my mom and I have become very close. They have better rooms and better meals than they ever had at my house. In my haste to reestablish a homestead and a place for me to be dad, I had chosen a house with some fundamental issues (no dishwasher, a septic system, and only one kid bedroom).

At this moment I'm in a converted single-car garage in the middle of a rich neighborhood. It's not bad. I'm not thrashing. But I have no privacy, no place to even think of establishing a relationship. And what's the first warning sign anyway? Someone with money troubles, or god forbid, no home.

In the divorce I am certain we were both doing the best we could. In the blindingly sad negotiations I agreed to giving up my request for 50/50 parenting, and I accepted the financial responsibility that would lock me into the big corporate track for the duration of the agreement (until my youngest child reached 18). What I didn't know in all these "good will" negotiations was that my soon-to-be-ex-wife would press the entire thing onto the state's attorneys.

She did it with little more than a reference to "looking after the children's interests." Um, sure, maybe, if I was doing something that demonstrated I was trying to skip out on my child support payments. That's when you go to the AG's office! Not as a normal course of business. And when the other person's home is threatened is the moment, I think, that you get real about the situation, you show some compassion for your co-parent, and you pause.

# Easier to Be Quiet

I know it would be easier for everyone if I would just shut up about my divorce. We've rehashed all the problems, all my perceived injustices, all the ways I've been wronged. I know I keep telling the same story, over and over. I know, I hear you.

And I won't shut up. Sorry.

In my marriage I learned to cope. I learned to nurture myself in the absence of love. I self-regulated and made do with less and less affection. But the education, the pattern that I learned about what love looked like, didn't begin with my ex. Nope, I learned how to be disinterested and disconnected from my parents, just as you probably did. I mean, they were the only examples we had. And boy did I learn how not to do a marriage. But of course, my images and imaginings were done by the time I was eight. It was all over by then, for my mom and dad. And everything else I thought I knew, I made up.

We are not ready for the changes of marriage. And we are certainly in no way prepared for parenting. It changes everything.

In my marriage, the changes were too much. We lost touch with one another and learned to be quiet even when we should be shouting at the top of our lungs, "This is hurting me."

Anger was a form of control in my family of origin. My father would rule his house with rage and yelling. And we would hide, tremble, and obey. But this is no way to behave. But what it did to our range of acceptable emotions was to limit our own access to anger. What it did for me was teach me to be agreeable, at all cost. To even lie if it meant I could avoid a fight.

But in a healthy relationship we need to fight. We need to have access to our full range of emotion. When I started getting angry about what wasn't working, I learned that it was okay. Of course, my ex would've loved me to stay in the submissive mode, as I started to draw boundaries for the first time in my marriage. I started expressing what wasn't working. I started to express my anger at being ignored emotionally and physically. And I demanded a change.

Of course, the change I was hoping for would've come in the form of realigning our marriage, and what I got was an exit request. But I was no longer willing to just be quiet.

So sure, I could shut up about the divorce, the depression, and the anger. And it would be a whole lot easier on all of us. But the beautiful thing about anger, that I did not know until I had unleashed some of it... Anger is healing and powerful.

Anger does not have to be abusive or rageful. Anger can be a consistent request for love and affection. Anger can be a demand for the other partner in a relationship to wake up and relearn how to express joy. Anger gave me back my balls, so I could express what I really needed in my marriage.

Try as I might, I was not able to call my ex back into love with me. Perhaps things had gone too far by the time I started fighting for my rights as a lover and husband. Perhaps my attention was no longer welcome. But I did not give up. I did not back down. I was no longer willing to masturbate alone all the time and wonder why she never had a sexual impulse. There, I said it. I wanted to have sex, and for some reason, she didn't.

And it wasn't the typical dude grabbing at his woman daily for gratification. It was not rutting sex I was after. I genuinely needed to feel skin-on-skin contact. I needed to affirm my warmth and closeness with my lover. I needed to be a lover and to reignite the lover in her.

I lost that negotiation. And ultimately I lost my marriage and the full access to my kids. Bummer. But I was not willing to just be quiet and bear the coldness and aloneness that my marriage had become. And while she ultimately was the person who asked for a divorce, I was the one who had finally begun speaking up. Even in the face of her divorce request, I was certain I was fighting for my marriage. I wasn't. I was fighting for what I wanted my marriage to return to, or what I'd hoped my marriage would become.

It's not easier to be quiet, actually. It's devastating not to speak your truth and be embraced. It's debilitating to ask again and again for affection and be given all number of reasons that it's not the right moment, or that I didn't ask in the right way. I was starving to death while lying next to the one person who could nourish me.

Well, fortunately I learned my lesson. And I am still embracing my ability to ask for what I need, to seek truth and connectedness, and to find another person who expresses herself easily through physical affection. It's simple when you both crave the same Love Language. It's a stretch and a negotiation if you don't. But it's never easier, in the long run, to be quiet.

# Reaching Forgiveness and Moving On After Divorce

It's been nine years and counting since my divorce began. It was finalized in August, but by this time I had left the house for the last time. While many things have remained the same, and the relationship with my ex is centered around the kids now, and not so much about our relationship, things still can trigger a painful memory or feeling of loss. Today was one of those times when dropping the kids' bags off at my old house and seeing a book on the kitchen counter was enough to spark a bit of WTF?

The book, *Passionate Marriage: Keeping Love and Intimacy Alive in Committed Relationships*, made me laugh at first. Then made me say, WTF? Then sort of made me feel bad for my ex who must be trying this time to form a healthy relationship with her boyfriend of over two years. But the book sort of ticked me off. I'm not exactly sure why. But the basic reaction was, "YEAH, that's a good one!"

After the knee jerk dickishness passed, I was a bit saddened by the idea.

1. That my ex would buy and read this book now, rather than when it could've had an impact on her marriage.

2. That my ex must be struggling with how to light up the passion with her boyfriend.

3. She must be hopeful of marriage and getting it right this time.

4.  And if she'd stayed IN this marriage, we would be working together to keep things passionate. As it was, I was the only one who seemed to think there was a problem.

How can I still be bitter about her decision to exit our marriage? Well, it's easy when you see the impact it has had on our kids and their ideas of stability and family. Sure, perhaps their perspectives are now more in alignment with reality, things change, love fades, and even divorce can rearrange things for the better, eventually, but it's gonna hurt real bad first.

Okay, so that's not a lot. And I'd have to say I am more grateful today that I am no longer in a passion-starved marriage. I am enjoying the first benefits of singlehood again and feeling fairly strong about my capabilities as a lover, potential mate, and even husband again. IF that's where we go. I am certainly also learning to question my need for that marriage. Today, I'm even asking questions about monogamy. I mean, what's the point? Couldn't we get a lot more energy and excitement by changing partners every once in a while?

Of course, that's not the way it worked for me. That's not the way I was wired. Today, I don't know. But I was fully committed to my marriage, and this woman now reading a book called *Passionate Marriage*. I was never doubting my desire or steadfast resolve. However, the truth is, I was unhappy.

They say the sign of a codependent relationship is how powerfully you wait and work for the other person to change. It doesn't work out. Some of the things I was beginning to howl about:

- Lack of affection

- Lack of touch of any kind

- Lack of sex

- Lack of financial partnership in the earning part of the business we had together

I learned, towards the end, when I withdrew my overbearing touch-love-joy energy from the relationship, there was nothing left. Zero energy was coming back. When the vacuum was created, I hoped she would wake up to the loss of playful affection and come back with some energy and affection of her own. That didn't happen at all. All that happened was the void of any feeling in our marriage became so clear, that even though I fought FOR the marriage over the next several months, I also knew I would not settle for anything less than a rejuvenated and passionate wife.

Something had been lost. Through the toil and tear of our relationship and the struggle of life, we had (she had) begun to shut down her passion. Though our relationship had begun with a lot of passion and touch and yes, sex, it was more of a one-way street during the last year of our marriage. I was always asking for a connection and always providing the way the caresses and the casual kisses. She had different priorities and was already withdrawing emotionally from our marriage.

As a divorced and emotionally available single parent, here are a few of the things I am finding again:

- Affection (If they don't dig you, don't do it. If they can't hold you and comfort you, don't do it.)

- The Love Language of Touch (Sure you can be with someone of a different language, but it's always going to be a compromise.)

- Sex that is open and fun (Healthy sex is an amazing thing. A woman who knows what she likes is another level beyond that. A woman who can teach me some things, and WOW.)

- Financial partnering doesn't come into play for a while, but it might in the long run.

- Pure friendship (Do you like being with the person? Do they engage your mind and your imagination?)

- Comparing notes on the experience of single parenting

- Desirability (There are women out there who find me attractive, who are not looking for rail-thin men in their 30s or even 40s. (I'm 51!)

- Mature women are more emotionally available and more

sexually open, and birth control is a non-issue. (Woohoo!)

With all those wonderful aspects of my new lease on life, I have to thank my ex-wife for the release. My own desires and unmet needs were causing me great pain. And that pain was probably not going to be met by her, unless she changed dramatically. Whatever caused her to change in the first place was probably not a quick fix, and certainly not something a book or counseling session was going to alleviate.

And with that, today, I give thanks to my ex-wife for actually having the balls to ask for a divorce. I would've limped along for the next several years, maybe forever, imagining, "This is as good as it gets."

Well, it's not. Things do get better. And the process of forgiveness and release is a continuous one. You don't wake up one day and you're healed, done, finished with your ex-partner. If you have kids, that road is going to go on for a long time. And you will need the other parent from time to time, and the best way to become a good co-parent is to heal yourself and move on. You will have good days, and fuck-you days, but as long as you keep returning to the process of release and move on, you will continue up the spiral of healing that leads to your next life. The post-divorce life that holds great riches.

# Waiting for the Other Person to Change – The Path Towards Divorce

[This was written as a response to a post on <u>DivorcedMoms.com</u>]

A lot of your story resonated with me, so I thought I would comment and share some perspective from the other side of the bed. Yep, you are waiting for your husband to change. And that's a trap, for both of you.

As the kid of an alcoholic dad, I got an early experience in AlAnon groups and Adult Children of Alcoholics groups as well. And one of the guiding principles is this: You cannot change the other person, you can only change yourself.

I hear that you are trying to act with compassion (in some aspects) and looking out for your girls. But I also hear your resentment and anger at your husband. I get it. You're pissed that he's not doing enough, that he continues his pattern of irresponsibility, and you are doing everything you can to revive a dead marriage. Um, well, I've got some good news and some bad news for you. He is never going to change. You on the other hand, can and have to change. It's all you can do. Everything else is wishful thinking, fantasy, and victimization.

More good news, you are not a victim of this marriage. You also have all the tools and resources at your disposal to help you through this, regardless of which path you take next.

Here's the part that's like me, the part I resonated with that's part of your husband's failure. You mention him taking the "just enough" approach to a lot of his responsibilities. And on a few of your examples, my mind was saying, "Oops, that's me too." Let me try to pull some of those issues apart, in hopes of illuminating some of my own dysfunctional thinking, but also to share some of my perspective, that it's not really a problem, it's the disagreement between the two of you that's the problem.

I am a "just in time" kind of person as well. I don't like to pay bills. But a few late payments don't really worry me either. When these issues came to light in my marriage, a lot of the friction was because we assumed we knew the other person's reasons for their behavior. I figured my then-wife was really uptight about money because she had come from a family of origin that struggled for money. I came from a background where money was not the issue, love and time was the issue in my early memories of my parents' marriage.

Okay, so I didn't mind paying a few bills late and possibly even letting a few go longer. This drove my partner crazy. Was I being irresponsible as she claimed? Was I refusing to grow up? Of course, those are perspectives about why I would think and act differently around bill paying, but they were not the answer. However, the resentment around this issue was much worse than the issue itself. A lot of energy was coming from my partner about bill paying. And the intensity of that emotional panic gave a lot of insight into how differently we saw the money issue, but mainly, it revealed a few of our "unspoken agreements."

She believed that if I loved her I would pay the bills with precision and promptness. I didn't connect the two items at all. For me bill paying was a pain in the ass, even if I had the money. She was very disciplined (maybe obsessed) about chores, and I was not. We could walk down the same hall day after day and I would never notice the burnt out lightbulb, yet every day she would get madder and madder that I was not a responsible or caring husband. Why? Because I was not changing the lightbulb. What?

We saw the world and the house in very different ways. It took a while to uncover a lot of these assumed agreements, which weren't agreements at all. In her mind, if I cared for her, I would change the lightbulb when it was burned out. Anything else demonstrated my irresponsibility and disdain for her priorities. That wasn't really it at all, I just didn't notice the damn lightbulb. And for her part, she was waiting for me to change, to notice things like lightbulbs and scruffy lawns, and just do the work. Just take care of it. Just fix it. "Just pay the damn bills on time."

Uncovering the assumed yet unspoken agreements is hard work. And while I am not saying this will change your husband into the caring and loving person you want, it might get to the core of what is bothering you.

Your initial reaction that things were over, that it was a dead relationship, however, is harder for me to fathom. And this is just the point that hit me the hardest. I read your title and kept the email in my inbox until I was ready to read it. See, I think my ex, also, decided at some point that things were over. She just failed to mention it to me.

And when you mention his addiction to porn, um, are you sure that's what's going on? Again, I can't possibly see into your relationship, but sometimes the "addiction" has more to do with sexual issues in the marriage, rather than his insatiable desire for 19-year-old porn stars. I'm guessing that as you decided he was a corpse in your house, your interest in sex with the dead man has been almost zero.

In my marriage we had periods of peak sexual connection and then nothing. The connecting activity of intimacy, even that didn't involve sex, came and went with the emotional tides of my partner. And when the tide was out, she rejected all offers, all invitations, all teases, all strokes, that MIGHT lead to intimacy. She exited the relationship emotionally, and one of the ways that showed up was in her lack of desire to connect with me on ANY PHYSICAL LEVEL. Nothing. Nada. She could go a month and never think of closeness.

Meanwhile, I was frustratedly pining away. And sure, I turned to porn. It was even a spoken agreement between us. When she was recovering from giving birth to each of our two kids, we went through the normal periods of asexual intimacy, and I would take care of myself in other ways. So I did, but it was no substitute for her or the real thing. It was cold, emotionless, release. And sure, people can get deep into it and addicted to all the varieties of fantasy that they might never act out in real life, but that wasn't my case.

But when she was healthy again, and we resumed our coupling, she would go through periods of coldness. And even that's normal, I get it. I understand that women are very different from men in their need for sexual release. It's something about testosterone levels. But when the woman shuts the passion down completely, something else is happening.

I can guess at what my wife's dysfunction was, but that would be silly. So much of sex and sexual intimacy is in our heads. To try to pull apart her lack of sexual desire, for me, would be a serious case of projection and bullshit. So I didn't do that. I asked nicely. I asked jokingly. I set aside special kid-free times. I did the dishes and bills more often. I looked for the lightbulbs that might be out. And guess what? Nothing worked. She was still closed for any form of closeness.

Okay, so now I can see this had something to do with me: she was mad about something, she was withholding intimacy because she was trying to get me to change, she was using intimacy as a tool. Bad idea. And she was having issues of her own: antidepressants maybe, overworked and overwhelmed maybe, unresolved anger issues with her family of origin. And of course, unresolved issues with me. But when the distance and anger goes on for days and weeks, the issue is much deeper than her and me. And it was. Or, I assume it was, I still don't know.

But in my experience the fracture and fallout at being placed in this emotional prison were horrible. I thrashed a little while trying to get things to change. I tried new things. I tried different ways of asking, connecting, nurturing. But again, that wasn't the issue. I could not make her change. I could not make her be someone else.

I realize, now, four years later, that I was just like the partner of an alcoholic, waiting for them to change. I am glad I was ultimately released from that unwinnable spiral of loss and frustration. For my kids' sake, I hope she's happy. I hope she figures it out with her new boyfriend. I really do. Because I don't want to see her in pain, even now. Even divorced, I want her to be happy. Her happiness is directly tied to my kids' experience of happiness and hope.

I learned my dependency in my family of origin. I was the little kid trying to be a hero, magician, football star, to get my dad to notice me and my value. I was trying to get him to stop drinking by being valuable enough as a son to be worthy of his attention. Of course, that's not how it works. That path never works.

Sorry to say it, but your story says to me that you are already gone. You say it yourself. And whatever has happened between you and your husband, with and without your therapist, is water under the bridge. Here's the rough part: He's not going to change.

But here's the win for you: You can and must change yourself. You are the only person you can influence. And you owe it to yourself and your daughters to get yourself healthy. Get the support you need. And do what YOU need to do. This state of dysfunction and living with your corpse-like husband is not likely to evolve into a healthy relationship. And a lot of it IS your perspective and YOUR unspoken agreements or wishes.

Speak now or forever hold your peace as you move along for the good of yourself and your daughters. Your husband will eventually have to take care of himself.

I wish you the best.

Sincerely,

*The Off Parent*

# My Divorce: A Searching and Fearless Moral Inventory

**Step 4 of AA: Make a searching and fearless moral inventory of ourselves.**

Today is a day of reflection. I am examining what I'm doing here on The Off Parent. Assessing the damage and progress of my self-observation, self-obsession, self-centered divorce blog. Let's see if we can get to the heart of the matter.

1. Strive to cut deep into the pain and healing of divorce recovery.
2. Express anger and hurt without blaming the other person.
3. Eliminate cynicism.
4. Always go for the truth, my truth, the painful truth.
5. Protect the innocent through anonymity and discretion.
6. Write for my own personal journey and healing; if there is a reader, that's fine, but I am not writing for anyone but myself.
7. Lift my psychology out of the hurt and sadness of depression and towards the healing and recovery for all the members of my family.
8. Do no harm.
9. Take on no more shame.

10.  Leave this discussion behind in favor of the next love and romance in my life.

Those are my goals. I'm not sure if I hit the mark with 100%, but that was (is) my intention. I have progressed from a confused and angry soon-to-be-ex-husband to a hopeful and romantic single father. That's the ultimate goal, and for that I give thanks.

## Writing is therapy.

For me, when I write down an experience, I begin to understand it in new ways. I find common threads with other experiences in my life. I hear echoes of past hurts. I recognize the hopeful little boy who survived a crappy divorce and has now grown into a divorce and family of my own. And here on these pages, sometimes, I process the hard stuff, I leave behind puddles of blood and anger that I no longer need. I am discarding these stories as fast as I can write them. Discharging the energy they might still hold on my emotional life, by putting down the bones of truth, as I remember it.

## I am not writing for you.

I am glad you are here. I have gotten a lot of support and love through the four years of writing my blog. I have been amazed by some of the comments, troubled by some of the misunderstand-ings, and encouraged to keep digging for gold. Digging for the heart of joy that is still inside that needs encouragement to hope and dream of loving again.

And I have found the language for that love again. I am writing aspi-rational love poems. There are still a few divorce poems, but for the most part, writing the blog transformed from angry/divorce/rant to relationship/love/discovery. Sure, there will always be flares of anger and sadness when managing the ongoing life of a single parent, but there are also great wins and joys that I am determined to celebrate here, right alongside the struggle.

## Next Steps

As I continue to change and challenge myself in the coming years,

I hope my blog and writing will continue to evolve with me. As I do find that next relationship, I hope that I can write with care and tenderness as "we," this woman and I, journey down the next road of our lives together.

As I grow and parent, writing will still be the rally point for my emotional triumphs and struggles. And as I struggle with depression or employment difficulties, I will also try to pull back the armor and release the dragons that still loom ahead for me.

In all cases, I thank you for coming along for the journey thus far. And if you have a comment, I value the feedback of my readers more than you can imagine. So tell me.

I hope you find love along your journey through whatever challenges you are facing. We can live through this shit together. And I will continue to light the way along my path so that you might learn from my trespasses and mistakes.

**Final note:** Why why why write about this painful stuff? My kids were five and seven when my then-wife decided for all of us that she was done with this marriage and wanted to move on to some other configuration. We are all still reeling from the fallout. Not all of it has been bad, but all of it has been transformative. I give thanks that she had the courage to step into the unknown and make the choice she thought was right for her and thus for all of us. Whatever the motivation or past, we are now a family in divorce. We have commitments and connections that will never cease between all of us. And in my attempts to heal myself, I hope to continue to be a positive influence on my kids' lives. We're in this together.

We need to evolve divorce and co-parenting to a higher discussion.

# WE CARRY ON. WE DO BETTER. WE KEEP GOING.

In divorce, you are still in a financial coupling. When I lost my job we all suffered. But that's not the moment to file against your former partner. I do think she's still mad at me, the same anger that infected our marriage. I'm not sure how that happens, or how someone dissipates it on their own. It takes work. And in a recent kid-focused therapy session her rage surfaced again, and I was again seeing the woman I have now gladly released. I don't need to be in any kind of relationship with someone who harbors such vitriol. And so we drop down into a logistics-and-money relationship. Sad. But maybe that's more accurate. That's kind of how the marriage had become as well.

# The Evolving Single Dad: Failure to Hopefulness Again

It's been over nine years since I walked out of my family home and changed everyone's life forever. Sounds dramatic now, but when I was going through it, I was not sure what the rest of my life held. There were moments I could not tell you one good thing that was ahead for me. And I cratered for a bit, taking refuge at my sister's house while I decided what I was going to do.

Now, looking back on it, the worst event I can recall in my personal history, I have somehow grown more resilient after having survived it. And I suppose my kids also have gained a bit of survival-in-the-face-of-the-storm strength. Today, even though I'm in a similar start-over place, I am not afraid or unhappy. I have taken a tumble as the result of my own actions, my own over-optimism, and the hostile ex. I have landed here. Starting over again. And there is hope here. The horizon is bright.

The evolution of The Off Parent has followed a similar trajectory. I have come from angry and vindictive to forgiveness and now letting go. Reaching this point offers some new opportunities. Rather than dealing with the Divorce, I am thinking more about Dating and what another relationship might look like. Rather than writing vitriolic screed, I'm leaning into love poems.

I have learned a lot on this path. I can say I am happy. I have learned to take even the catastrophic failure and flip it around into opportunity. And then somehow continue to see the hope in that opportunity. There really is a wide range of paths out of this moment of pause. There is no reason to thrash. I will reemerge when the next job provides the means to support both myself and my kids. Until then, I'm going to enjoy this moment to the fullest. I'm recommitting to tennis and fitness. I'm starting to sing songs again.

When you're flat on your back in depression and failure, what you learn is how to get back up. And inside that "how" is the hope that is self-generated and self-sustaining. Hope is the key. Without it, the daily grind is brutal and even the smiling pictures of your children don't lift you. But if you can imagine a single hopeful idea, cling to it, set it on fire, and tend the hopefulness. You can find the energy again to reach out for what you need by building and nurturing the hopefulness in yourself.

# The Infinitely Desirable Woman with the Fractured Soul

She was walking across the parking lot this woman, my ideal physical type. (Perhaps more of a cultural archetype) Tall, model-thin, dark hair, dark skin, and slightly disheveled. And an alcoholic.

How do I know? She was heading into an AA meeting, at 9:30 a.m. on a Wednesday.

What is it about the devilishly distraught woman that calls to our heroic hearts? What caregiver gene is responsible for this longing for the vacant and damaged woman? There must be something in my past that causes me to reach out, even if only in my mind, for this beauty in distress.

Ah, I got it.

She is my sister. My sister who was ten years old when I was born. My sister who raised me like her child, or doll, or "baby buddha brother," as she used to call me. Ah, that hurts.

My sister committed suicide when she was in her early thirties. She was so brilliant and beautiful, though. And so creative, talented, and loving. When she threw herself from the bridge on Christmas day, our whole family grieved on so many levels. We're still recovering from her death today.

Today, I didn't see my sister walking across the parking lot. I saw a metaphor. A cliché. I saw a fractured woman, who was also strikingly attractive, with an undertow. I've become leery of that undertow. If the attraction is too visceral… If I want her just a tad too much… I have to go back to the drawing board and try to understand what is going on inside me that is calling out such a strong emotional reaction.

I long to fall in love. I crave the free fall. But I know that often this euphoria is more like a drug than an actual signal for the beginning of a healthy relationship. Crap. I don't want to worry about healthy relationships. I want heat. I want magic. I want the drug.

There was nothing beyond her beauty today that triggered this response in me. Well, that and my loneliness for companionship. Okay, maybe I miss my sister. Sure. Maybe that's the love someone is supposed to feel for their moms. Well, my "mom" was really my sister. My singing, dancing, gypsy sister.

I'm not sad talking about her. I'm sad understanding that my soul still craves something that is missing of her love. Some closeness, and openness, that I have never experienced again. Something that I saw in my first relationship post-divorce. Some part of that first post-divorce girlfriend who could easily express her love for me. Nothing to deliver. No expectations. Just love.

What is pure love? We understand it sometimes in terms of how we feel about our pets. They are pure love, because they love us unconditionally. They are dependent on us and wait for us to reappear when we leave.

Somehow, today, I realized I am still waiting for my sister to reappear. Not in physical form (holy cow, that's either zombie talk, or ghost talk, and I'm not a fan of either), but in feeling. I'm hungry for someone to love, to love with an unhinged abandon. I'm ready to fall.

And even noticing this tendency towards the edge, towards someone I know would be toxic, given my history, I can still feel the pull towards this woman as she meanders into the halls of recovery. I am not actually craving her, or even her body type. I've grown more aware, recently, of how programmed we have become by the fashion and marketing industries to crave the Victoria's Secret image. I don't. I don't anymore. I used to. I still feel the rise and pull. But I can walk away from that trap, with the same firmness I continue to my car and drive back to my office.

See, I was in my own therapy this morning. I'm in my own recovery. Not from drugs or alcohol, but from something that might make those addictions much easier. This morning I was in counseling for my own health and welfare. Almost like a coach. But I don't have a life coach. Almost like an AA meeting, but I don't have an addiction (unless you call this proclivity towards unavailable women an addiction).

I'm getting better on all fronts. I'm healing, day by day. And, in some ways, I'm still healing from the loss of my loving sister. She comes out in my unhealthy desire for the fractured soul of the disheveled woman.

Let's leave that dishevelment alone. In our relationships, let's not look for a person who needs our help, and not a person who can help us, either. Let us look for happy, healthy, and balanced. Everything within reason, right?

Today, I salute my sister and her beauty. And I salute Victoria's Secret models and the woman crossing the parking lot to attend to her own healing.

I'd prefer something a little less dangerous and perhaps a little less racy.

# *please stay gone (a poem)*

i can't take it back
you've got it
our love has spawned
these beautiful
beautifuls

and when you've got them
i am ultimately alone
alone in an ultimate way
a way i never anticipated
as we looked ahead
our mad plans
and said
i
do

today
i don't
and i can't imagine
what misguided joy caused you
to send me photos
happy photos
i guess you're showing me
"our kids" are so happy

but
why

are you in any of the pictures

so i can put you up on my mantle
if i had a mantle

please leave yourself out
your smile still hurts
the ache now is for them
and the loss of any seconds
with them
you were my world
you are gone
please stay gone

thank you

# Divorce Support: For the Children *and* the Parents

We need to dispense with the pleasantries right up front.

- Divorce is an awful hardship for everyone in the fracturing family.
- With two professional parents, the man is likely to make more money.
- Two homes cost more than twice as much, for the person paying child support.
- Child support is not an entitlement, even if the law and the benefactor might see it this way.
- The financial bindings of the family exist long past 18 years of age.
- Both parents deserve food, clothing, and shelter.
- When adversity strikes, both parents are affected.
- 50/50 parenting after divorce is not the norm.
- If your former partner struggles for a few years after divorce, with emotional issues, financial issues, etc., this is an opportunity for continued compassion, not legal action.
- Some fathers will be assholes and try to get out of paying child support or (in the case of 50/50 custody) their fair share of the expenses.
- 50/50 custody and a 50/50 financial split actually keeps the

father closer to the family.

- If you married and parented 50/50, regardless of how you feel about the divorce, regardless of which side you were on (stay married or leave), you should work together towards a 50/50 divorce.

You can't ask for primary custody and then start complaining about having too many parenting responsibilities. Well, you can, but the argument says more for 50/50 custody than it does for your obvious hardship. Of course, you complained during our marriage that I didn't do enough. Didn't pay the bills right, didn't mow the lawn enough, didn't put the dishes in the dishwasher every night before heading to bed.

So we're divorced. And in the eyes of the law you are the custodial parent. It's what you wanted. I'm sure you had your reasons, I'm sure you could've told the judge, with a straight face, how you do all the parenting. But you know it's not true. Not even close.

Let's say you get married and both of you work. In the negotiations for how kids will be possible, you both decide that the mom will work significantly less, so that the kids have their mom with them at all times. As they enter school, perhaps you will start back to work, so we can share that load again. And we may decide that you will still meet the bus at 3:00 every weekday, but it's a privilege, not a chore. It's a benefit, not a burden.

So when the grand *consul de divorce* asks, "So how do you share the parenting duties now?" You can answer, I'm the primary caregiver. And I know you honestly believed it. Well, okay, maybe a tad of it was vindictive and defensive. I mean, you had to say that to even begin the discussions at anything other than 50/50 custody. How old school.

Falling back on the line, "It's what she will get if you go to court," I was handed the options. Non-custodial parent, Standard Possession Order, and a hefty child support payment.

But wait... Didn't we agree to the parenting arrangements? And now It's being used against me? Didn't we agree to a cooperative divorce?

How is this cooperative, when you come out of the gate asking for well over half?

If I had really gone the cooperative route, I would've hired an attorney right at the beginning as well. She did. Instead, I put my faith in the counselor, and in the good will of the mother of my children. I was wrong, or misguided, on both counts.

Here's the situation. When the court awards custodial and noncustodial roles, a nice child-support formula kicks in. That's how the state likes it. Somebody is going to pay. And in your decree, if you are as lucky as I am, you will have a document that even allows the court to garnish your wages first, before your take-home pay. The message is this. You cannot be trusted to pay in a timely manner. And even if you are having financial difficulties, the child support payments come first.

I don't argue that my kids deserve the full benefit of both of our salaries. But when I lost one of my primary clients, and was about to slip into a late-payment status, my ex-wife pushed everything into the Attorney General's office. Putting my livelihood at risk and preventing me from taking any measures to save my house. She didn't care about me or my house. She wanted the money. She was entitled to it. Obviously. It was right there in writing. I signed the decree. What was I arguing about?

I wasn't arguing. I was pleading. "Please don't do this. I am not trying to hide any money. I am looking to replace the client. I am looking for a job, to leave the consulting practice I had built over the  last four years. Just hold off. There is no need to bring the state's lawyers into this."

Here, filing our case with the AG's office was akin to her shouting "Fuck you." Of course, that's my opinion. And, of course, she is entitled to her money. That's the law.

But what is the law of human dignity? What does compassion for your co-parent mean? At this very moment, my attorney tells me, the AG's office could have my ass thrown in jail for failure to pay child support. A criminal? How cooperative is that?

As we moved closer to AG day, I was asking my ex-wife to understand my situation. "Don't you think a father also deserves a place to live, and the electricity and cell phone service to continue gainful employment?" She answered, "I don't know what you want me to answer to that."

Um... What I wanted her to do was not file suit against me with the State of Texas and turn me into a deadbeat dad. What I wanted was to keep the house I had fought so hard to buy and afford, just barely scraping by, even in the good times. What I wanted was a tiny bit of compassion. "Just pause for a second and think about what you're doing. Do you think it's going to help the situation by filing suit against me? Do you think that will make me work harder, or look for a job harder?"

No answer.

And she filed. And now I'm a deadbeat dad. I'm lucky. My mom (yep, 51 and living with mom) had some spare rooms in her house. At least my kids have rooms to sleep in when it's my time. But did she think of the consequences of taking legal action against me? Did she imagine how that might damage my credit? Might take my house out from under me? That it might even show up in my background checks as I'm looking so desperately for those full-time jobs that would afford me both a place to live and her child support checks?

I don't know what she was thinking. I don't really know what she thinks today. She's still hoppin' mad about something. The money. My 50/50 effort in getting the kids to doctor's appointments, after-school activities, etc. She's just mad. But she's been mad at me for years. At least one full year before she divorced me. So she's gonna be mad. That's a fact of life. I hope she gets better. But I can't count on that.

I've had fantastic interviews all summer long. Five of them turned into final-round negotiations. And I still haven't gotten the offer. Hmm. I'm not sure what's in that background check. I'm hoping that her AG action did not put a "do not hire" mark in my file. But I guess I won't know.

Anyway, it's a long road back to having a BIG CORP job and a happy home. Even getting back into a house, now, is going to be a long way off. She took... Wait, it was my fault. I should've done better. It's a long way back. And I'm not sure she would've fired off the final "Press Charges" missile had she known her actions would damage my ability to pay her the money she was demanding.

It's all okay. We're going to make it. All of us. Her too. She sent pictures tonight of her and the kids at the beach. (That was our family vacation.) I'm not sure what her motivation was at sending me pictures of HER with the kids. Maybe it's motivation to get a job and get back into the swing of paying for her vacations with the kids. (Sorry, that was bitter and sarcastic.) I'm sure she was just sending me happy pictures along with her happy thoughts of me getting that next big job. I think that's what she wanted all along. Maybe that was even the unconscious reason she divorced me.

Onward and upward. I've been asked to a full-day interview next week with a company I'm very excited about. This is my fourth full-day interview this summer. How do I get a look at that "background" file?

# Isn't Dad's House Also Important in Divorce?

There is something amazing about being cut free from all of your worldly possessions. It's a bit disorienting. I remember the first year without a house, when most of my "stuff" was in my old garage, her garage. We had agreed that she would keep the house, and I would get some of the retirement savings she had socked away while we were married. While the financial split was equitable, the appreciation of the house and the penalties of early withdrawal from retirement accounts were not really factored in. Oh well, water under the bridge.

Well, last week was an amazing succession of unfortunate events.

1.  The AG's office took control of my banking account.
2.  My storage unit (since I'm homeless again, at the moment) auctioned off all of my "stuff" for a $350 late payment.

Today I am finally untethered completely. I guess if I were in a negative state of mind I would be taking this much harder. But somehow, even the "stuff" feels like a release. But I might be in shock. The loss of all of my books, all of my music recording equipment, all of my furniture, the bulk of my clothing, everything, leaves me a bit like I was when I first left the marital house. Very lean and not-so-mean. But I'm prepared to get meaner.

Let's not forget, that in divorce BOTH parents have to have a place to live. Both parents need food, electricity, wifi, and the means to make a living, or continue to hunt for the next job, as the case may be.

I am not certain my wife had thought through the ramifications of the divorce. She was not concerned about MY house. Why should she be? Once divorced, it was not her problem.

Except, it is. See, if she wants to have a dad who is able to remain in the kids' lives, she has to understand that, for better or worse, we are still attached financially. The only problem is, if you don't keep this perspective in mind, you might think child support is an entitlement. **You might begin to imagine that child support supersedes food and shelter for the other parent.** And in the eyes of the law, you might be correct. But in the eyes of your kids...

That's where the rub is. You should not be willing to file against your ex-partner when they are trying to find work, when they are remaining attached and available, when they are sharing all the information they have about prospects, timing, and money. If your co-parent is doing everything they can to get back on their feet, why oh why would you then file with the Attorney General's office to enforce the divorce decree? There is nothing to get. The AG's office got $1,200 on Thursday.

Now, my fault is not figuring out how to deal with the AG's office sooner. I was advised by my attorney to pay her something. But in the months since I lost my house, my income has been almost nil. I've made $4,500 in consulting fees, but the rest of my food and living expenses have been covered by a loan from my mom. An ongoing loan that I ask for and renegotiate monthly. And of course, it comes with intense scrutiny and baggage.

My job search has been aggressive and fruitful but has not produced the required salary that would support my child support obligation AND a place to live. At this point, even an apartment is out of reach. And if I can't figure out a path forward with the AG's office, I suppose I'm going to jail.

My guess is that my ex-wife would not have wanted me to go to jail. But she didn't show any remorse about the embarrassment of the

AG's lien against me on Thursday, or the fact that this shut down 100% of my financial options for the long holiday weekend.

We lean on family in times like these. And I am grateful that my mom has not only a place for me and my kids to live but also a little money to help me get through this moment between a rock and hard place. But I'm feeling the squeeze.

When my kids leave their mom's house, it is expected that I can shelter, feed, and entertain them. But when my ex-wife filed against me with the AG's office, I was showing her my income, talking to her openly about my financial issues, essentially showing her all of my cards. And even when I was negotiating with the mortgage company to reset my mortgage, and she was aware that I was trying to do this to keep the house, she filed.

On the same day she asked, "How's it going with the house," which might sound like a friendly encouragement, she also told me she'd "turned it all over to the AG's office."

Today, stripped of my house and of all but my bed and a few clothes, I am lean and getting mean. I'm not sure what options are available to me today. But as things get better, and I get stronger, I'm going to revisit the entire agreement between us.

Starting with my court-ordered weekends. I'm going to ask we go back to 1st, 3rd, and 5th weekends again. I gave them up to allow my ex-wife to sync her schedule with her boyfriend's schedule. Well, since his kid is now off to college, it shouldn't matter to her. But to me, it's the possibility of an extra weekend about four or five times a year.

Dad's house is important. Please remember this. If you are fighting to hurt your ex, your fighting WILL hurt your kids. As you strike a blow of entitlement, you are also stripping away some of the trust and goodwill you both agreed to in cooperating during the divorce process.

Well, I am proof that you can co-parent with a gun to your head, but it's a lot harder. And I can only imagine how at that moment when I was nearly begging for compassion, she must've been holding onto some anger, some vindictiveness that prevented her from seeing the kids' experience of what she was about to do. But I can't imagine doing the same, had the tables been turned. If you are still angry with your ex, you need to get that anger out in other ways. Rousing the "enforcement" of the state has dire consequences. And there was no "enforcement" to be had. Even in seizing my account last week, she is no closer to getting the monthly support payments back on schedule. But she has thrown me, and thus the kids when they are with me, back a year or more in this journey back home.

I initiated some talks this summer to see if "birdnesting" in the house might be an option. It was at the request of the kids. During one of the first sessions, my ex got so angry, lit up the room with her fury, about how I was not doing my part of the parenting, with doctor's appointments, and dental appointments, and etc. Her list I am sure was as endless as it had been when we were married. Except I am not the cause of her anger. She's responsible for her own ongoing anger issues.

I was happy to have a counselor in the room to settle things back to reality. And the next day I let the counselor know I wasn't going to be pursuing the bird nesting. I don't ever need to open myself up to that rage again, about anything.

**Update:** I saw my Asteroids machine for sale on Craigslist. So asked them if I could get some of my personal items. Here's how they responded.

> we r so sorry, but we did not have the ability to take everything, so a lot of the personal items went to the dumpster - and most of the books r sold already, as that is one of the things we can sell back to online book stores relatively quick and easy - however if there is anything that u can thing of that u would really like back we would b glad to look for it - my wife is putting together a box with a few items that u might like - she mentioned an award and some pictures we still have - again sorry we don't have much left, but we had no way to store it all so we had to let most of it go

**Update #2:** this was hard, but at least positive.

This one almost got thrown, but it's still here

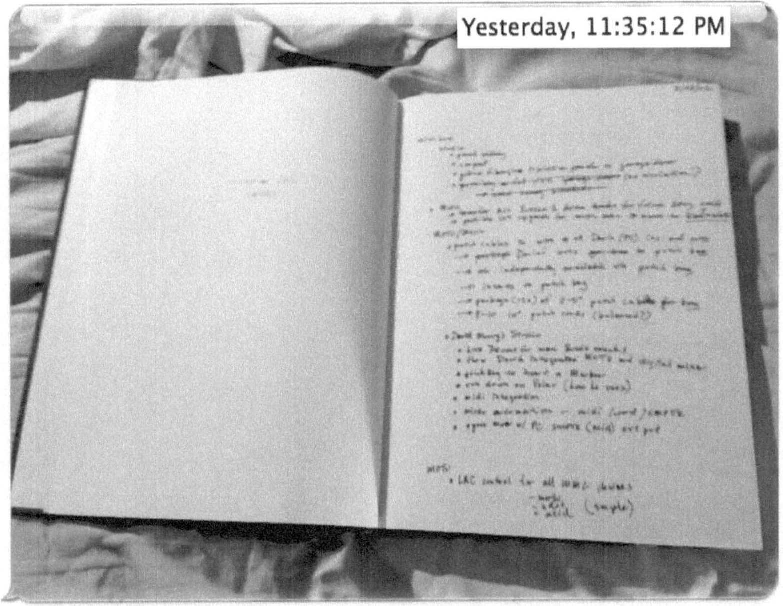



Not sure if there's any more cause most were not kept

I am meeting the gentleman and his wife this afternoon to recover some of the personal items that they couldn't sell. They are also selling me back my printer and a hard drive. It feels like something out of Risky Business. "Never fuck with another man's empire, Joel."

Hopeful, happy, and upward.

# Happy Mom Chat About How I Got Here: What I Figured Out

*[The October before I lost the house, I had a wonderful email back from Arianna Huffington. The Huffington Post was going to pick up and publish my new 100% Positive Single Parenting blog. (see http://wholeparent.org) I knew I wasn't going to get rich or famous as a result of this new venture, but just having this new recognition of the work I was doing to turn the negative potential of divorce into something that I could share publicly and proudly was a real win. I was excited. My ex-wife, of course, was not. She asked me not to write anything about her or the kids, ever. It was a real moment of agreeing to disagree.*

*This entry sort of paves the way toward the future. I'll see you there.]*

I took lunch to my mom's house today, just to stop by and say hi. We talked about this blog for a bit.

See my ex left some sort of message about something I was doing that was damaging my family. My mom wanted to know what it was. I showed her The Off Parent and explained how it was anonymous.

"But it's on Facebook," she said.

"Yes, but it's not connected to me in any way. I don't even LIKE my own page."

She was happy with my explanation. And she said something next that brought the conversation to a different place.

"I'm glad to see you taking a different path than your father."

She went on to tell me about how he once told her she was the reason he drank. "So, I told him I wouldn't be that reason any more."

We talked about my dad and how he went on to marry another drinker and eventually drank himself and her to death. And I told her that her survival after the divorce had colored a lot of my childhood and probably formed a good portion of my personality. She was always quoted as saying, "I'm turning X's into plusses." And that's kind of a maxim that I have learned to live by.

Even as things got hard for us, back in my elementary through high school years, she would keep us pointed at the good side of the situation. A lot of the time I thought it was bullshit. Just a way of escaping some of the pain of the moment. But eventually I heard myself using the exact same phrase when talking to myself about bad situations.

I told my mom about how this blog had given me a voice, a place to process the anger and frustration at the divorce. And how eventually those parts of the blog began to subside and a new part of the story began to emerge. As I transitioned out of anger, depression, and divorce mechanics, I started moving into how to turn this major X into a major WIN.

The divorce is the biggest thing that's ever happened in my life, and I'm 50 years old. What ripped through my safety and joy has now become the fire that has burned away the bullshit and brought me down to WHAT'S IMPORTANT.

Here's what I figured out about the positive side of this blog, and the positive part of the divorce, for me.

**1. Self-Care.** Physical and mental health are a full-time process for me. While I've never had a substance problem, I have used the 12-step program for various parts of my recovery. What I am working on is EMOTIONAL SOBRIETY.

**2. Kids First.** There is nothing in my life more important than the love and support of my children. Keeping them safe from the bitterness and anger that could've erupted in my divorce was always part of my agreement with their mom.

**3. 100% Positive.** While there are plenty of times I'm angry with their mom, there is NEVER any reason to voice those complaints to my kids. I remember how horrible my dad was at speaking about my mom. And of course, she was doing only a little better at voicing the victim side of the horror. And it was pretty bad. Eventually, in high school my dad began taking it out on me, saying that the divorce was my fault and saying that I didn't love him. These will never be words that my kids hear from me. And I believe the ex has the same intention.

**4. Lead With Love.** I may not be in love with their mother, but I will never stop loving her. It's often that love that turns to bitterness and hate when it's flipped around. But I won't ever go there. She is gone. She is someone else's. And I can do better each day remembering the relationship of the divorce is about my kids. And if she's happier, they will benefit.

I don't always get it right, but I keep trying to return to these principles. And as my ex has now turned me over to the Attorney General's office, I guess we will see what it's like trying to abide by these principles while she is suing me. I imagine that she is doing the best she knows how. At least, I suppose, she will know with the bankruptcy that I'm filing, that I'm not secretly stashing money away, or trying to keep her from child support payments.

Even in cutting off most of the conversation between us, I think she must be doing that for some personal, self-preservational reasons, rather than hate for me. We've got these great kids. And we do everything we can to support and encourage them. If she no longer wants to sit face-to-face to map out some plans with me, that's okay. I guess we go back to emailing each other. That worked some while we were married.

And I'll keep mapping my own path along this journey here. Turning my ex into a plus.